Rip Foster
Rides the Gray Planet

By

BLAKE SAVAGE

Illustrated by

E. DEANE CATE

WILDSIDE PRESS

www.wildsidepress.com

CONTENTS

Major Barris Faced Rip and the New Planeteers

RIP FOSTER
Rides the Gray Planet

CHAPTER ONE

SCN SCORPIUS, SPACEBOUND

A thousand miles above earth's surface the great space platform sped from daylight into darkness. Once each two hours it circled the earth completely, spinning along through space like a mighty wheel of steel and plastic.

Through a telescope from earth the platform seemed a lifeless, lonely disk, but within it, hundreds of spacemen and Planeteers went about their work.

In a ready-room at the outer edge of the platform, a Planeteer officer faced a dozen slim, black-clad young men who wore the single golden orbits of lieutenants. This was a graduating class, already commissioned, having a final, informal get-together.

The officer, who wore the three-orbit insignia of a major, was lean and trim. His hair was cropped short, like a gray fur skull cap. One cheek was marked with the crisp whiteness of an old radiation burn.

"Stand easy," he ordered briskly. "The general instructions of the Special Order Squadrons say that it's my duty as senior officer to make a farewell speech. I intend to make a speech if it kills me—and you, too."

The dozen new officers facing him broke into grins. Major Joe Barris had been their friend, teacher, and senior officer during six long years of training on the space platform. He could no more make a formal speech than he could breathe high vacuum, and they all knew it.

Lieutenant Richard Ingalls Peter Foster, whose initials had given him the nickname of "Rip," asked, "Why don't you sing us a song instead, Joe?"

Major Barris fixed Rip with a cold eye. "Foster, three orbital turns, then front and center."

Rip obediently spun around three times, then walked forward and stood at attention, trying to conceal his grin.

"Foster, what does SOS mean?"

"Special Order Squadrons, sir."

"Right. And what else does it mean?"

"It means, 'Help!' sir."

"Right. And what else does it mean?"

"Superman or simp, sir."

This was a ceremony in which questions and answers never changed. It was supposed to make Planeteer cadets and junior officers feel properly humble, but it didn't work. By tradition, the Planeteers were the cockiest gang that ever blasted through high vacuum.

Major Barris shook his head sadly. "You admit you're a simp, Foster. The rest of you are simps, too. But you don't believe it. You've finished six years on the platform. You've made a few little trips out into space. You've landed on the moon a couple times. So now you think you're seasoned space spooks. Well, you're not. You're simps."

Rip stopped grinning. He had heard this before. It was part of the routine. But he sensed that this time Joe Barris wasn't kidding.

The major rubbed the radiation scar on his cheek absently as he looked them over. They were like twelve chicks out of the same nest. They were all about the same size, a compact five-feet-eleven inches, 175 pounds. They wore loose black tunics, belted over full trousers which gathered into white cruiser boots. The comfortable uniforms concealed any slight differences in build. The twelve were all lean of face, with hair cropped to the regulation half inch. Rip was the only redhead among them.

"Sit down," Barris commanded. "I'm going to make a farewell speech."

Rip pulled a plastic stool toward him. The others did the same. Major Barris remained standing.

"Well," he began soberly, "you are now officers of the Special Order Squadrons. You're Planeteers. You are lieutenants by order of the Space Council,

Federation of Free Governments. And—space protect you!—to yourselves, you're supermen. But never forget this: to ordinary spacemen, you're just plain simps. You're trouble in a black tunic. They have about as much use for you as they have for leaks in their air locks. Some of the spacemen have been high-vacking for twenty years or more, and they're tough. They're as nasty as a Callistan *teekal*. They like to eat Planeteer junior officers for breakfast."

Lieutenant Felipe "Flip" Villa asked, "With salt, Joe?"

Major Barris sighed. "No use trying to tell you space-chicks anything. You're lieutenants now, and a lieutenant has the thickest skull of any rank, no matter what service he belongs to."

Rip realized that Barris had not been joking, no matter how flippant his speech. "Go ahead," he urged. "Finish what you were going to say."

"Okay. I'll make it short. Then you can catch the Terra rocket and take your eight earth-weeks leave. You won't really know what I'm talking about until you've batted around space for a while. All I have to say adds up to one thing. You won't like it, because it doesn't sound scientific. That doesn't mean it isn't good science, because it is. Just remember this: when you're in a jam, trust your hunch and not your head."

The twelve stared at him, open-mouthed. For six years they had been taught to rely on scientific

methods. Now their best instructor and senior officer
was telling them just the opposite!

Rip started to object, then he caught a glimmer
of meaning. He stuck out his hand. "Thanks, Joe.
I hope we'll meet again."

Barris grinned. "We will, Rip. I'll ask for you as
a platoon commander when they assign me to cleaning up the goopies on Ganymede." This was the
major's idea of the worst Planeteer job in the Solar
System.

The group shook hands all around; then the
young officers broke for the door on the run. The
Terra rocket was blasting off in five minutes, and
they were due to be on it.

Rip joined Flip Villa and they jumped on the
high speed track that would whisk them to Valve
Two on the other side of the platform. Their gear
was already loaded. They had only to take seats on
the rocket and their six years on the space platform
would be at an end.

"I wonder what it will be like to get back to high
gravity?" Rip mused. The centrifugal force of the
spinning platform acted as artificial gravity, but it
was considerably less than earth's.

"We probably won't be able to walk straight until
we get our earth-legs back," Flip answered. "I wish
I could stay in Colorado with you instead of going
back to Mexico City, Rip. We could have a lot of
fun in eight weeks."

Rip nodded. "Tough luck, Flip. But anyway, we have the same assignment."

Both Planeteers had been assigned to Special Order Squadron Four, which was attached to the cruiser *Bolide*. The cruiser was in high space, beyond the orbits of Jupiter and Saturn doing comet research.

They got off the track at Valve Two and stepped through into the rocket's interior. Two seats just ahead of the fins were vacant and they slid into them. Rip looked through the thick port beside him and saw the distinctive blue glow of a nuclear drive cruiser sliding sternward toward the platform.

"Wave your eye stalks at that job," Flip said admiringly. "Wonder what it's doing here?"

The space platform was a refueling depot where conventional chemical fuel rockets topped off their tanks before flaming for space. The newer nuclear drive cruisers had no need to stop. Their atomic piles needed new neutron sources only once in a few years.

The voice horn in the rocket cabin sounded. "The *SCN Scorpius* is passing Valve Two, landing at Valve Eight."

"I thought that ship was with Squadron One on Mercury," Rip recalled. "Wonder why they pulled it back here?"

Flip had no chance to reply because the chief rocket officer took up his station at the valve and began to call the roll. Rip answered to his name.

The rocket officer finished the roll, then announced: "Buttoning up in twenty seconds. Blast off in forty-five. Don't bother with acceleration harness. We'll fall free, with just enough flame going for control."

The ten-second warning bell sounded, and, before the bell had ceased, the voice horn blasted. "Get it! Foster, R.I.P., Lieutenant. Report to the platform commander. Show an exhaust!"

Rip leaped to his feet. "Hold on, Flip. I'll see what the old man wants and be right back."

"Get flaming," the rocket officer called. "Show an exhaust like the man said. This bucket leaves on time, and we're sealing the port."

Rip hesitated. The rocket would leave without him!

Flip said urgently, "You better ram it, Rip."

He knew he had no choice. "Tell my folks I'll make the next rocket," he called, and ran. He leaped through the valve, jumped for the high speed track and was whisked around the rim of the space platform.

He ran a hand through his short red hair, a gesture of bewilderment. His records had cleared. So far as he knew, all his papers were in order, and he had his next assignment. He couldn't figure why the platform commander would want to see him. But the horn had called "show an exhaust," which meant to get there in a hurry.

He jumped off the track at the main crossrun and hurried toward the center of the platform. In a moment he stood before the platform commander's door, waiting to be identified.

The door swung open and a junior officer in the blue tunic and trousers of a spaceman motioned him to the inner room. "Go in, Lieutenant."

"Thank you." He hurried into the commander's room and stood at attention.

Commander Jennsen, the Norwegian spaceman who had commanded the platform since before Rip's arrival as a raw cadet, was dictating into his command relay circuit. As he spoke, printed copies were being received in the platform personnel office, Special Order Squadron headquarters on earth, aboard the cruiser *Bolide* in high space, and aboard the newly landed cruiser *Scorpius*.

Rip listened, spellbound.

"Foster, R.I.P., Lieutenant, SOS. Serial seven-nine-four-three. Assigned SOS Four. Change orders, effective this date-time. Cancel earth-leave. Subject officer will report to commander, *SCN Scorpius* with detachment of nine men. Senior non-commissioned officer and second in command, Koa, A.P., Sergeant-major, SOS. Serial two-nine-four-one. Commander *Scorpius* will transport detachment to coordinates given in basic cruiser astrocourse, delivering orders to detachment enroute. Take full steps for maximum security. This is Federation priority A, Space Council security procedures."

Rip swallowed hard. The highest possible priority, given by the Federation itself, had cancelled his leave. Not only that, but the cruiser to which he was assigned was instructed to follow Space Council security procedures, which meant the job, whatever it was, was rated even more urgent than secret!

Commander Jennsen looked up and saw Rip. He snapped, "Did you get all of that?"

"Y-Yessir."

"You'll get written copies on the cruiser. Now flame out of here. Collect your men and get aboard. The *Scorpius* leaves in five minutes."

Rip ran. The realization hit him that the big nuclear cruiser had stopped at the platform for the sole purpose of collecting him and nine enlisted Planeteers.

The low gravity helped him cover the hundred yards to the personnel office in five leaps. He swung to a stop by grabbing the push bar of the office door. He yelled at the enlisted spaceman on duty, "Where do I find nine men?"

The spaceman looked at him vacantly. "What for? You got a requisition, Lieutenant?"

"Never mind requisitions," Rip snapped. "I've got to find nine Planeteers and get them on the *Scorpius* before it flames off."

The spaceman's face cleared. "Oh. You mean Koa's detachment. They left a few minutes ago."

"Where? Where did they go?"

The spaceman shrugged. The doings of Planeteers were no concern of his. His shrug said so.

Rip realized there was no use talking further. He ran down the long corridor toward the outer edge of the platform. The enlisted men's squadrooms were near Valve Ten. So was the supply department. His gear had departed on the Terra rocket, and he couldn't go to space with only the tunic on his back. He swung to the high speed track and braced himself as it sped him along the platform's rim.

There was no moving track inward to the enlisted Planeteers' squadrooms. He legged it down the corridor in long leaps, muttering apologies as blue-clad spacemen and cadets moved to the wall to let him pass.

The squadrooms were on two levels. He looked in the upper ones and found them deserted. The squads were on duty somewhere. He ran for the ladder to the lower level, took the wrong one, and ended up in a snapper-boat port. He had trained in the deadly little fighting rockets, and they never failed to interest him. But there wasn't time to admire them now. He went back up the ladder with two strong heaves, found the right ladder, and dropped down without touching. His knees flexed to take up the shock. He came out of the crouch facing a black-clad Planeteer sergeant who snapped to rigid attention.

"Koa," Rip barked. "Where can I find him?"

"He's not here, sir. He and eight men left fifteen minutes ago. I don't know where they went, sir."

Rip shot a worried glance at his wrist chronometer. He had two minutes left before the cruiser departed. No more time now to search for his men. He hoped the sergeant-major had sense enough to be waiting at some sensible place. He went up the ladder hand over hand and sped down the corridor to the supply room.

The spaceman first class in charge of supplies was turning an audio-mag through a hand viewer, chuckling at the cartoons. At the sight of Rip's flushed, anxious face he dropped the machine. "Yessir?"

"I need a spack. Full gear including bubble."

"Yessir." The spaceman looked him over with a practiced eye. "One full space pack. That would be medium-large, right, sir?"

"Correct." Rip took the counter stylus and inscribed his name, serial number, and signature on the blank plastic sheet. Gears whirred as the data was recorded.

The spaceman vanished into an inner room and reappeared in a moment lugging a plastic case called a space pack, or "spack" for short. It contained complete personal equipment for space travel. Rip

grabbed it. "Fast service. Thanks, Rocky." All spacemen were called "Rocky" if you didn't know their
names. It was an abbreviation for rocketeer, a title
all of them had once carried.

Valve Eight was some distance away. Rip decided
a cross ramp would be faster than the moving track.
He swung the spack to his shoulder and made his
legs go. Seconds were ticking off, and he had an
idea the *Scorpius* would make space on time, whether or not he arrived. He lengthened his stride and
rounded a turn by going right up on the wall,
using a powerful leg thrust against a ventilator tube
for momentum.

He passed an observation port as he reached the
platform rim and caught a glimpse of ruddy rocket
exhaust flames outlined against the dark curve of
earth. That would be the Terra rocket making its
controlled fall to home with Flip aboard. Without
slowing, he leaped across the high speed track, nar-
rowly missing a senior space officer. He shouted
his apologies, and gained the entrance to Valve
Eight just as the high buzz of the radiation warning sounded, signaling a nuclear drive cruiser pre-
paring to take off.

Nine faces of assorted colors and expressions
turned to him. He had a quick impression of black
tunics and trousers. He had found his detachment!
Without slowing, he called, "Follow me!"

The cruiser's safety officer had been keeping an

eye on the clock, his forehead creased in a frown as he saw that only a few seconds remained to departure time. He walked to the valve opening and looked out. If his passengers were not in sight, he would have to reset the clock.

Rip went through the valve opening at top speed. He crashed head-on into the safety officer.

The safety officer was driven across the deck, his arms pumping for balance. He grabbed at the nearest thing, which happened to be the deputy cruiser commander.

The pre-set control clock reached firing time. The valve slid shut and the take-off bell reverberated through the ship.

And so it happened that the spacemen of the *SCN Scorpius* turned their valves, threw their controls and disengaged their boron control rods, and the great cruiser flashed into space, while the deputy commander and the safety officer were completely tangled with a very flustered and unhappy new Planeteer lieutenant.

Sergeant-major Koa and his men had made it before the valve closed. Koa, a seven-foot Hawaiian, took in the situation and said crisply in a voice all could hear, "I'll bust the bubble of any son of a space sausage who laughs!"

CHAPTER TWO

RAKE THAT RADIATION!

The deputy commander and the safety officer got untangled and hurried to their posts with no more than black looks at Rip. He got to his feet, his face crimson with embarrassment. A fine entrance for a Planeteer officer, especially one on his first orders!

Around him, the spacemen were settling in their acceleration seats or snapping belts to safety hooks. From the direction of the stern came a rising roar as liquid methane dropped into the blast tubes, flaming into pure carbon and hydrogen under the terrible heat of the atomic drive.

Rip had to lean against the acceleration. Fighting for balance, he picked up his spack and made his way to the nine enlisted Planeteers. They had braced against the ship's drive by sitting with backs against bulkheads, or by lying flat on the magnesium deck. Sergeant-major Koa was seated against a vertical brace, his brown face wreathed in a grin as he waited for his new officer.

Rip looked him over carefully. There was a saying among the Planeteers that an officer was only as good as his senior sergeant. Koa's looks were reassuring. His face was good-humored, but he had a solid jaw and a mouth that could get tough when necessary. Rip wondered a little at his size. Big men usually didn't go to space; they were too subject to space sickness. Koa must be a special case.

Rip slid to the floor next to the sergeant-major and stuck out his hand. He sensed the strength in Koa's big fist as it closed over his.

Koa said, "Sir, that was the best *fleedle* I've ever seen an earthling make. You been on Venus?"

Rip eyed him suspiciously, wondering if the big Planeteer was laughing at him. Koa was grinning, but it was a friendly grin. "What is a *fleedle?*" Rip demanded. "I've never been on Venus."

"It's the way the water-hole people fight," Koa explained. "They're like a bunch of rubber balls when they get to fighting. They ram each other with their heads."

Rip searched his memory for data on Venus. He couldn't recall any mention of *fleedling*. Venusians, if his memory was right, had a sort of blowgun as a main weapon. He told Koa so.

The sergeant-major nodded. "That's when they mean business, Lieutenant. *Fleedling* is more like us fighting with our fists. Sort of a sport. Great Cosmos! The way they dive at each other is something to see."

Rip grinned. "I didn't know I was going to *fleedle* those officers. It isn't the way I usually enter a cruiser." He hadn't entered many. He added, "I suppose I ought to report to someone."

Koa shook his head. "No use, sir. You can't walk around very well until the ship reaches brenn-schluss. Besides, you won't find any space officers who'll talk to you."

Rip stared. "Why not?"

"Because we're Planeteers. They'll give us the treatment. They always do. When the commander of this bucket gets good and ready, he'll send for you. Until then, we might as well take it easy." He pulled a bar of Venusian *chru* from his pocket. "Have some. It will make breathing easier."

The terrific acceleration made breathing a little uncomfortable, but it was not too bad. The chief effect was to make Rip feel as though a ton of invisible feathers were crushing him against the vertical brace. He accepted a bite of the bittersweet vegetable candy and munched thoughtfully. Koa seemed to take it for granted that the spacemen would give them a rough time.

He asked, "Aren't there any spacemen who get along with the Special Order Squadrons?"

"Never met one." Koa chewed *chru*. "And I was on the *Icarus* when the whole thing started."

Rip looked at him in surprise. Koa didn't seem that old. The bad feeling between spacemen and the Special Order Squadrons had started about 18 years ago when the cruiser *Icarus* had taken the first Planeteers to Mercury.

He reviewed the history of the expedition. The spacemen's job had been to land the newly created Special Order Squadron on the hot planet. The job of the squadron was to explore it. Somehow, confusion developed and the spacemen, including the officers, later reported that the squadron had instructed them to land on the sun side of Mercury, which would have destroyed the spaceship and its crew, or so they believed at the time.

The commanding officer of the squadron denied issuing such an order. He said his instructions were to land as close to the sun side as possible, but not on it. Whatever the truth—and Rip believed the SOS version, of course—the crew of the *Icarus* mutinied, or tried to. They made the landing on Mercury with squadron guns pointed at their heads. Of course, they found that a sun-side landing wouldn't have hurt the ship. The whole affair was pretty well hushed up, but it produced bad feeling between the Special Order Squadrons and the spacemen. "Trigger happy space bums," the spacemen called them, and much worse besides.

The men of the Special Order Squadrons, searching for a handy nickname, had called themselves Planeteers, because most of their work was on the planets. As Major Joe Barris had told the officers of Rip's class, "You might say that the spacemen own space, but we Planeteers own everything solid that's found in it."

The Planeteers were the specialists—in science, exploration, colonization, and fighting. The spacemen carried them back and forth, kept them supplied, and handled their message traffic. The Planeteers did the hard work and the important work. Or so they believed.

To become a Planeteer, a recruit had to pass rigid intelligence, physical, aptitude, and psychological tests. Less than 15 out of each 100 who applied were chosen. Then there were two years of hard training on the space platform and the moon before a recruit was finally accepted as a Planeteer private. Out of each 15 who started training, an average of five fell by the wayside.

For Planeteer officers, the requirements were even tougher. Only one out of each 500 applicants finally received a commission. Six years of training made them proficient in the techniques of exploration, fighting, rocketeering, and both navigation and astrogation. In addition, each became a full-fledged specialist in one field of science. Rip's specialty was astrophysics.

Sergeant-major Koa continued, "That business on the *Icarus* started the war, but both sides have been feeding it ever since. I have to admit that we Planeteers lord it over the spacemen like we were old man Cosmos himself. So they get back at us with dirty little tricks while we're on their ships. We command on the planets, but they command in space. And they sure get a great big nuclear charge out of commanding us to do the dirty work!"

"We'll take whatever they hand us," Rip assured him, "and pretend we like it fine." He gestured at the other Planeteers. "Tell me about the men, Koa."

"They're a fine bunch, sir. I hand-picked them myself. The one with the white hair is Corporal Nels Pederson. He's a Swede. I served with him at Marsport, and he's a real rough space spickaroo in a fight. The other corporal is little Paulo Santos. He's a Filipino, and the best snapper-boat gunner you ever saw."

He pointed out the six privates. Kemp and Dowst were Americans. Bradshaw was an Englishman, Trudeau a Frenchman, Dominico an Italian, and Nunez a Brazilian.

Rip liked their looks. They were as relaxed as acceleration would allow, but you got the impression that they would leap into action in a microsecond if the word were given. He couldn't imagine what kind of assignment was waiting, but he was satisfied with his Planeteers. They looked capable of anything.

He made himself as comfortable as possible, and encouraged Koa to talk about his service in the Special Order Squadrons. Koa had plenty to tell, and he talked interestingly. Rip learned that the big Hawaiian had been to every planet in the system, had fought the Venusians on the central desert, and had mined nuclite with SOS One on Mercury. He also found that Koa was one of the 17 pure-blooded Hawaiians left. During the three hours that acceleration kept them from moving around the ship, Rip got a new view of space and of service with the SOS—it was the view of a Planeteer who had spent years around the Solar System.

"I'm glad they assigned you to me," Rip told Koa frankly. "This is my first job, and I'll be pretty green, no matter what it is. I'll depend on you for a lot of things."

To his surprise, Koa thrust out his hand. "Shake, Lieutenant." His grin showed strong white teeth. "You're the first junior officer I ever met who admitted he didn't know everything about everything. You can depend on me, sir. I won't steer you into any meteor swarms."

Koa had half turned to shake hands. Suddenly he spun on around, his head banging against the deck. Rip felt a surge of loosened muscles that had been braced against acceleration. At the same time, silence flooded in on them with an almost physical shock. He murmured, "brennschluss," and the murmur was like a trumpet blast.

The *Scorpius* had reached velocity and the nuclear drive had cut out. From terrific acceleration they had dropped to zero. The ship was making high speed, but velocity cannot be felt. For the moment, the men were weightless.

A near-by spaceman had heard Rip's comment. He spoke in an undertone to the man nearest. His voice was pitched low enough so Rip couldn't object officially, but loud enough to be heard.

"Get this, gang. The Planeteer officer knows what brennschluss is. He doesn't look old enough to know which end his bubble goes on."

Rip started to his feet, but Koa's hand on his arm restrained him. With a violent kick the big sergeant-major shot through the air. His line of flight took him by the spaceman, and somehow their arms got linked. The spaceman was jerked from his post and the two came to a stop against the ceiling.

Koa's voice echoed through the ship. "Sorry. I'm not used to no-weight. Didn't mean to grab you. Here, I'll help you back to your post."

He whirled the helpless spaceman like a bag of feathers and slung him through the air. The force of the action only flattened Koa against the ceiling, but the hapless spaceman shot forward head first and landed with a clang against the bulkhead. He didn't hit hard enough to break any bones, but he would carry a bump around on his head for a day or two.

Koa's voice floated after him. "Great Cosmos! I sure am sorry, spaceman. I guess I don't know my own strength." He kicked away from the ceiling, landing accurately at Rip's side. He added in a hard voice all could hear, "They sure are a nice gang, these spacemen. They never say anything about Planeteers."

No spaceman answered, but Koa's meaning was clear. No spaceman had better say anything about the Planeteers! Rip saw that the deputy commander and the safety officer had appeared not to notice the incident. Technically, there was no reason for an officer to take action. It had all been an "accident." He smiled. There was a lot he had to learn about dealing with spacemen, a lot Koa evidently knew very well indeed.

Suddenly he began to feel weight. The ship was going into rotation. The feeling increased until he felt normally heavy again. There was no other sensation, even though the space cruiser now was spinning on its axis through space at unaltered speed. The centrifugal force produced by the spinning gave them an artificial gravity.

Now that he thought about it, brennschluss had come pretty early. The trip apparently was going to be a short one. Brennschluss . . . funny, he thought, how words stay on in a language even after their original meaning is changed. Brennschluss was German for "burn out." It was rocket talk, and it meant the moment when all the fuel in a rocket burned out. It had come into common use because the English "burn out" also could mean that the engine itself had burned out. The German word meant only the one thing. Now, in nuclear drive ships, the same word was used for the moment when power was cut off.

Words interested him. He started to mention it to Koa just as the telescreen lit up. An officer's face appeared. "Send that Planeteer officer to the commander," the face said. "Tell him to show an exhaust."

Rip called instantly to the safety officer. "Where's his office?"

The safety officer motioned to a spaceman. "Show him, Nelson."

Rip followed the spaceman through a maze of passages, growing more weightless with each step. The closer to the center of the ship they went, the less he weighed. He was pulling himself along by plastic pull cords when they finally reached the door marked "Commander."

The spaceman left without a word or a salute. Rip pushed the lock bar and pulled himself in by grabbing the door frame. He couldn't help thinking it was a rather undignified way to make an entrance.

Seated in an acceleration chair, a safety belt across his middle, was Space Commander Keven O'Brine, an Irishman out of Dublin. He was short, as compact as a deto-rocket, and obviously unfriendly. He had a mathematically square jaw, a lopsided nose, green eyes, and sandy hair. He spoke with a pronounced Irish brogue.

Rip started to announce his name, rank, and the fact that he was reporting as ordered. Commander O'Brine brushed his words aside and stated flatly, "You're a Planeteer. I don't like Planeteers."

Rip didn't know what to say, so he kept still. But sharp anger was rising inside of him.

O'Brine went on, "Instructions say I'm to hand you your orders enroute. They don't say when. I'll decide that. Until I do decide, I have a job for you and your men. Do you know anything about nuclear physics?"

Rip's eyes narrowed. He said cautiously, "A little, sir."

"I'll assume you know nothing. Foster, the designation SCN means Space Cruiser, Nuclear. This ship is powered by a nuclear reactor. In other words, an atomic pile. You've heard of one?"

Rip controlled his voice, but his red hair stood on end with anger. O'Brine was being deliberately insulting. This was stuff any new Planeteer recruit knew. "I've heard, sir."

"Fine. It's more than I had expected. Well, Foster, a nuclear reactor produces heat. Great heat. We use that heat to turn a chemical called methane into its component parts. Methane is known as marsh gas, Foster. I wouldn't expect a Planeteer to know that. It is composed of carbon and hydrogen. When we pump it into the heat coils of the reactor, it breaks down and creates a gas that burns and drives

"You're a Planeteer. I Don't Like Planeteers."

us through space. But that isn't all it does."

Rip had an idea what was coming, and he didn't like it. Nor did he like Commander O'Brine. It was not until much later that he learned that O'Brine had been on his way to Terra to see his family for the first time in four years when the cruiser's orders were changed. To the commander, whose assignments had been made necessary by the needs of the Special Order Squadrons, it was too much. So he took his disappointment out on the nearest Planeteer, who happened to be Rip.

"The gases go through tubes," O'Brine went on. "A little nuclear material also leaks into the tubes. The tubes get coated with carbon, Foster. They also get coated with nuclear fuel. We use thorium. Thorium is radioactive. I won't give you a lecture on radioactivity, Foster. But thorium mostly gives off the kind of radiation known as alpha particles. Alpha is not dangerous unless breathed or eaten. It won't go through clothes or skin. But when mixed with fine carbon, thorium alpha contamination makes a mess. It's a dirty mess, Foster. So dirty that I don't want my spacemen to fool with it.

"I want you to take care of it instead," O'Brine said. "You and your men. The deputy commander will assign you to a squadroom. Settle in, then draw equipment from the supply room and get going. When I want to talk to you again, I'll call for you. Now blast off, Lieutenant, and rake that radiation.

Rake it clean."

Rip forced a bright and friendly smile. "Yes, sir," he said sweetly. "We'll rake it so clean you can see your face in it, sir." He paused, then added politely, "If you don't mind looking at your face, sir—to see how clean the tubes are, I mean."

Rip turned and got out of there.

Koa was waiting in the passageway outside. Rip told him what had happened, mimicking O'Brine's Irish accent.

The sergeant-major shook his head sadly. "This is what I meant, Lieutenant. Cruisers don't clean their tubes more'n once in ten accelerations. The commander is just thinking up dirty work for us to do, like I said."

"Never mind," Rip told him. "Let's find our squadroom and get settled, then draw some protective clothing and equipment. We'll clean his tubes for him. Our turn will come later."

He remembered the last thing Joe Barris had said, only a few hours before. Joe was right, he thought. To ourselves we're supermen, but to the spacemen we're just simps. Evidently O'Brine was the kind of space officer who ate Planeteers for breakfast.

Rip thought of the way the commander had turned red with rage at that crack about his face, and resolved, "He may eat me for breakfast, but I'll try to be a good, tough mouthful!"

CHAPTER THREE

Commander O'Brine had not exaggerated. The residue of carbon and thorium on the blast tube walls was stubborn, dirty, and penetrating. It was caked on in a solid sheet, but when scraped, it broke up into fine powder.

The Planeteers wore coveralls, gloves, and face masks with respirators, but that didn't prevent the stuff from sifting through onto their bodies. Rip, who directed the work and kept track of the radiation with a gamma-beta ion chamber and an alpha proportional counter, knew they would have to undergo personal decontamination.

He took a reading on the ion chamber. Only a few milliroentgens of beta and gamma radiation. That was the dangerous kind, because both beta particles and gamma rays could penetrate clothing and skin. But the Planeteers wouldn't get enough of a dose to do any harm at all. The alpha count was high, but so long as they didn't breathe any of the dust it was not dangerous.

The *Scorpius* had six tubes. Rip divided the Planeteers into two squads, one under his direction and one under Koa's. Each tube took a couple of hours'

36

hard work. Several times during the cleaning the men would leave the tube and go into the main mixing chamber while the tube was blasted with live steam to throw the stuff they had scraped off out into space.

Each squad was on its last tube when a spaceman arrived. He saluted Rip. "Sir, the safety officer says to secure the tubes."

That could mean only one thing: deceleration. Rip rounded up his men. "We're finished. The safety officer passed the word to secure the tubes, which means we're going to decelerate." He smiled grimly. "You all know they gave us this job just out of pure love for the Planeteers. So remember it when you go through the control room to the decontamination chamber."

The Planeteers nodded enthusiastically.

Rip led the way from the mixing chamber through the heavy safety door into the engine control room. His entrance was met with poorly concealed grins by the spacemen.

Halfway across the room Rip turned suddenly and bumped into Sergeant-major Koa. Koa fell to the deck, arms flailing for balance—but flailing against his protective clothing. The other Planeteers rushed to pick him up, and somehow all their arms and hands beat against each other.

The protective clothing was saturated with fine dust. It rose from them in a choking cloud, was picked up, and dispersed by the ventilating system. It was contaminated dust. The automatic radiation safety equipment filled the ship with an ear-splitting buzz of warning. Spacemen clapped emergency respirators to their faces and spoke unkindly of Rip's Planeteers in the saltiest space language they could think of.

Rip and his men picked up Koa and continued their march to the decontamination room, grinning under their respirators at the consternation around them. There was no danger to the spacemen since they had clapped on respirators the moment the warning sounded. But even a little contamination meant the whole ship had to be gone over with instruments, and the ventilating system would have to be cleaned.

The deputy commander met Rip at the door of the radiation room. Above the respirator, his face looked furious.

"Lieutenant," he bellowed. "Haven't you any more sense than to bring contaminated clothing into the engine control room?"

Rip was sorry the deputy commander couldn't see him grinning under his respirator. He said innocently, "No, sir. I haven't any more sense than that."

The deputy grated, "I'll have you up before the Discipline Board for this."

Rip was enjoying himself thoroughly. "I don't think so, sir. The regulations are very clear. They say, 'It is the responsibility of the safety officer to insure compliance with all safety regulations both by complete instructions to personnel and personal supervision.' Your safety officer didn't instruct us and he didn't supervise us. You better run him up before the Board."

The deputy commander made harsh sounds into his respirator. Rip had him, and he knew it. "He thought even a stupid Planeteer had sense enough to obey radiation safety rules," he yelled.

"He was wrong," Rip said gently. Then, just to make himself perfectly clear, he added, "Commander O'Brine was within his rights when he made us rake radiation. But he forgot one thing. Planeteers know the regulations, too. Excuse me, sir. I have to get my men decontaminated."

Inside the decontamination chamber, the Planeteers took off their masks and faced Rip with admiring grins. For a moment he grinned back, feeling pretty good. He had held his own with the spacemen, and he sensed that his men liked him.

"All right," he said briskly. "Strip down and get into the showers."

In a few moments they were all standing under the chemically treated water, washing off the contaminated dust. Rip paid special attention to his hair, because that was where the dust was most likely to stick. He had it well lathered when the water suddenly cut off. At the same moment, the

cruiser shuddered slightly as control blasts stopped
its spinning and left them all weightless. Rip saw
instantly what had happened. He called, "All right,
men. Down on the floor."

The Planeteers instantly slid to the shower deck.
In a few seconds the pressure of deceleration pushed
at them.

"I like spacemen," Rip said wryly. "They wait
until just the right moment before they cut the
water and decelerate. Now we're stuck in our birth-
day suits until we land—wherever that may be."

Corporal Nels Pederson spoke up in a soft Stock-
holm accent. "Never mind, sor. Ve'll get back at
them. Ve alvays do!"

While the *Scorpius* decelerated and started maneuvering for a landing, Rip did some rapid calculations. He knew the acceleration and deceleration
rates of cruisers of this class measured in terms of
time, and part of his daily routine on the space platform had been to examine the daily astro-plot which
gave the positions of all planets and other large
bodies within the solar system.

There was only one possible destination: Mars.

Rip's pulse quickened. He had always wanted to
visit the red planet. Of course he had seen all the
films, audio-mags, and books on the planet, and he
had tried to see the weekly spacecast. He had a good
idea of what the planet was like, but reading or

viewing was not like actually landing and taking a look for himself.

Of course they would land at Marsport. It was the only landing area equipped to handle nuclear drive cruisers.

The cruiser landed and deceleration cut to zero. At the same moment, the water came on.

Rip hurriedly finished cleaning up, dressed, then took his radiation instruments and carefully monitored his men as they came from the shower. Private Dowst had to go back for another try at getting his hair clean, but the rest were all right. Rip handed his instruments to Koa. "You monitor Dowst when he finishes. I want to see what's happening."

He hurried from the chamber and made his way down the corridors toward the engine control room. There was a good possibility he might get a call from O'Brine, with instructions to take his men off the ship. He might finally learn what he was assigned to do!

As he reached the engine control room, Commander O'Brine was giving instructions to his spacemen on the stowage of equipment that evidently was expected aboard. Rip felt a twinge of disappointment. If the *Scorpius* had landed to take on supplies of some kind, his assignment was probably not on Mars.

He started to approach the commander with a question about his orders, then thought better of it.

He stood quietly near the control panel and watched.

The air lock hissed, then slid open. A Martian stood in the entryway, a case on his shoulder. Rip watched him with interest. He had seen Martians before, on the space platform, but he had never gotten used to them. They were human, still . . .

He tried to figure out, as he had before, what it was that made them strange. It wasn't the blue-whiteness of their skins nor the very large, expressionless eyes. It was something about their bodies. He studied the Martian's figure carefully. He was slightly taller and more slender than the average earthman, but his chest measurements would be about the same. Nor were his legs very much longer.

Suddenly Rip thought he had it. The Martian's legs and arms joined his torso at a slightly different angle, giving him an angular look. That was what made him look like a caricature of a human. Although he was human, of course. As human as any of them.

Rip saw that other Martians were in the air lock, all carrying cases of various sizes and shapes. They came through into the control room and put them down, then turned without a word and hurried back into the lock. They were all breathing heavily, Rip noticed. Of course! The artificial atmosphere inside the space ship must seem very heavy and moist to them after the thin, dry air of Mars.

The lock worked and the Martians were replaced

by others. They, too, deposited their cases. But these cases were bigger and heavier. It took four Martians to carry one, which meant they weighed close to half a ton each. The Martians could carry more than double an earthman's capacity.

When the lock worked next time, a Planeteer captain came in. He breathed the heavy air appreciatively, fingering the oxygen mask he had to wear outside. He saluted Commander O'Brine and reported, "This is all, sir. We filled the order exactly as Terra sent it. Is there anything else you need?"

O'Brine turned to his deputy. "Find out," he ordered. "This is our last chance. We have plenty of basic supplies, but we may be short of audio-mags and other things for the men." He turned his back on the Planeteer captain and walked away.

The captain grinned at O'Brine's retreating back, then walked over to Rip. They shook hands.

"I'm Southwick, SOS Two. Canadian."

Rip introduced himself and said he was an American. He added, "And aside from my men, you're the first human being I've seen since we made space."

Southwick chuckled. "Trouble with the spacemen? Well, you're not the first."

Talking about assignments wasn't considered good practice, but Rip was burning with curiosity. "You don't by chance know what my assignment is, do you?"

The captain's eyebrows went up. "Don't you?"

Rip shook his head. "O'Brine hasn't told me."

"I don't know a thing," Southwick said. "We got instructions to pack up a pretty strange assortment of supplies for the *Scorpius* and that's all I know. The order was in special cipher, though, so we're all wondering about it."

The deputy commander returned, reported to O'Brine, then walked up to Rip and Southwick. "Nothing else needed," he said curtly. "We'll get off at once."

Southwick nodded, shook hands with Rip, and said in a voice the deputy could hear, "Don't let these spacemen bother you. Trouble with them is, they all wanted to be Planeteers and couldn't pass the intelligence tests." He winked, then hurried to the air lock.

Spacemen worked quickly to clear the deck of the new supplies, stowing them in a near-by workroom. Within five minutes the engine control room was clear. The safety officer signaled and the radiation warning sounded. Taking off!

Rip hurried to the squadroom and climbed into an acceleration chair. The other Planeteers were already in the room, most of them in their bunks. Koa slid into the chair beside him. "Find out anything, sir?"

"Nothing useful. A bunch of equipment came aboard, but it was in plain crates. I couldn't tell what it was."

Acceleration pressed them against the chairs. Rip sighed, picked up an audio-circuit set, and put it over his ears. Might as well listen to what the circuit had to offer. There was nothing else to do. Music was playing, and it was the kind he liked. He settled back to relax and listen.

Brennschluss came some time later. It woke Rip up from a sound sleep. He blinked, glancing at his chronometer. Great Cosmos! With that length of acceleration they must be high-vacking for Jupiter! He waited until the ship went into the gravity spin, then got out of his chair and stretched. He was hungry. Koa was still sleeping. He decided not to wake him. The sergeant-major would see that the men ate when they wanted to.

In the messroom only one table was occupied— by Commander O'Brine.

Rip gave him a civil hello and started to sit alone at another table. To his surprise, O'Brine beckoned to him.

"Sit down," the spaceman invited gruffly.

Rip did, and wondered what was coming next.

"We'll start to decelerate in about ten minutes," O'Brine said. "Eat while you can." He signaled and a spaceman brought Rip the day's ration in an individual plastic carton with thermo-lining. The Planeteer opened it and found a block of mixed vegetables, a slab of space-meat, and two units of biscuit. He wrinkled his nose. Space-meat he didn't

mind. It was chewy but tasty. The mixed vegetable
ration was chosen for its food value and not for taste.
A good mouthful of earth-grass would be a lot more
palatable. He sliced off pieces of the warm stuff and
chewed thoughtfully, watching O'Brine's face for a
clue as to why the commander had invited him to
sit down.

It wasn't long in coming. "Your orders are the
strangest things I've ever read," O'Brine stated. "Do
you know where we're going?"

Rip figured quickly. They had accelerated for six
and a half hours. Now, ten minutes after brennschluss, they were going to start deceleration. That
meant they had really high-vacked it to get somewhere in a hurry. He calculated swiftly.

"I don't know exactly," he admitted. "But from   ·
the ship's actions, I'd say we were aiming for the
far side of the asteroid belt. Anyway, we'll fall short
of Jupiter."

There was a glimmer of respect in O'Brine's
glance. "That's right. Know anything about asteroids, Foster?"

Rip considered. He knew what he had been taught
in astronomy and astrogation. Between Mars and
Jupiter lay a broad belt in which the asteroids swung.
They ranged from Ceres, a tiny world only 480
miles in diameter, down to chunks of rock the size
of a house. No accurate count of asteroids—or minor
planets, as they were called—had been made, but

the observatory on Mars had charted the orbits of over 100,000. Most of them were only a mile or two in diameter. Others, much smaller, had never been charted by anyone. One leading astronomer had estimated that as many as 50,000 asteroids filled the belt.

"I know the usual stuff about them," he told O'Brine. "I haven't any special knowledge."

O'Brine blinked. "Then why did they assign you? What's your specialty?"

"Astrophysics."

"That might explain it. Second specialty?"

"Astrogation." He couldn't resist adding, "That's what scientists call space navigation, Commander."

O'Brine started to retort, then apparently thought better of it. "I hope you'll be able to carry out your orders, Lieutenant," he said stiffly. "I hope, but not much. I don't think you can."

Rip asked, "What are my orders, sir?"

O'Brine waved in the general direction of the wall. "Out there, somewhere in the asteroid belt, Foster, there is a little chunk of matter about one thousand yards in diameter. A very minor planet. We know its approximate coordinates as of two days ago, but we don't know much else. It happens to be a very important minor planet."

Rip waited, intent on the commander's words.

"It's important," O'Brine continued, "because it happens to be pure thorium."

Rip gasped. Thorium! The rare, radioactive element just below uranium in the periodic table of the elements, the element used to power this very ship! "What a find!" he said in a hushed voice. No wonder the job was Federation priority A, with Space Council security! "What do I do about it?" he asked.

O'Brine grinned. "Ride it," he said. "Your orders say you're to capture this asteroid, blast it out of its orbit, and drive it back to earth!"

CHAPTER FOUR

Rip walked into the squadroom with a copy of the orders in his hand. After one look at his face, the Planeteers clustered around him. Santos woke those who were sleeping, while Rip waited.

"We have our orders, men," he announced. Suddenly he laughed. He couldn't help it. At first he had been completely overcome by the responsibility, and the magnitude of the job, but now he was getting used to the idea and he could see the adventure in it. Ten wild Planeteers riding an asteroid! Sunny space, what a great big thermo-nuclear stunt!

Koa remarked, "It must be good. The lieutenant is getting a real atomic charge out of it."

"Sit down," Rip ordered. "You'd better, because you might fall over when you hear this. Listen, men. Two days ago the freighter *Altair* passed through the asteroid belt on a run from Jupiter to Mars." He sat down, too, because deceleration was starting. As his men looked at each other in surprise at the quickness of it, he continued, "The old bucket found something we need. An asteroid of pure thorium."

The enlisted Planeteers knew as well as he what that meant. There were whistles of astonishment.

49

Koa slapped his big thigh. "By Gemini! What do we do about it, sir?"

"We capture it," Rip said. "We blast it loose from its orbit and ride it back to earth."

He sat back and watched their reactions. At first they were stunned. Trudeau, the Frenchman, muttered to himself in French. Dominico, the Italian, held up his hands and exclaimed, "Santa Maria!"

Kemp, one of the American privates, asked, "How do we do it, sir?"

Rip grinned. "That's a good question. I don't know."

That stopped them. They stared at him. He added quickly, "Supplies came aboard at Marsport. We'll get the clue when we open them. Headquarters must have known the method when they assigned us and ordered the equipment."

Koa stood up. He was the only one who could have moved upright against the terrific deceleration. He walked to a rack at one side of the squadroom and took down a copy of "The Space Navigator." Then, resuming his seat, he looked questioningly at Rip. "Anything else, sir? I thought I'd read what there is about asteroids."

"Go ahead," Rip agreed. He sat back as Koa began to recite what data there was, but he didn't listen. His mind was going ten astro units a second. He thought he knew why he had been chosen for the job. Word of the priceless asteroid must have reached headquarters only a short time before he was scheduled to leave the space platform. He could imagine the speed with which the specialists at Terra base had acted. They had sent orders instantly to the fastest cruiser in the area, the *Scorpius,* to stand by for further instructions. Then their personnel machines must have whirred rapidly, electronic brains searching for the nearest available Planeteer officer with an astrophysics specialty and astrogation training.

He could imagine the reaction when the machine turned up the name of a brand-new lieutenant. But the choice was logical enough. He knew that most, if not all, of the Planeteer astrophysicists were either in high or low space on special work. Chances are there was no astrophysicist nearer than Ganymede. So the choice had fallen to him.

He had a mental image of the Terra base scientists feeding data into the electronic brain, taking the results, and writing fast orders for the men and supplies needed. If his estimate was correct, work at the Planeteer base had been finished within an hour of the time word was received.

When they opened the cases brought aboard by the Martians, he would see that the method of blasting the asteroid into a course for earth was all figured out for him.

Rip was anxious to get at those cases. Not until he saw the method of operation could he begin to figure his course. But there was no possibility of getting at the stuff until brennschluss. He put the problem out of his mind and concentrated on what his men were saying.

". . . and he slugged into that asteroid going close to seven AU's," Santos was saying. The little Filipino corporal shrugged expressively.

Rip recognized the story. It was about a supply ship, a chemical drive rocket job that had blasted into an asteroid a few years before.

Private Dowst shrugged, too. "Too bad. High vack was waiting for him. Nothing you can do when Old Man Nothing wants you."

Rip listened, interested. This was the talk of old space hands. They had given the high vacuum of empty space a personality, calling it "high vack," or "Old Man Nothing." With understandable fatalism, they believed—or said they believed—that when high vacuum really wanted you, there was nothing you could do.

Rip had come across an interesting bit of word knowledge. Spacemen and Planeteers alike had a way of using the phrase, "By Gemini!" Gemini, of course, was the constellation of the Twins, Castor and Pollux. Both were useful stars for astrogation. The Roman horse soldiers of ancient history had sworn, "By Gemini," or "By the Twins." The Romans believed the stars were the famous Greek warriors Castor and Pollux, placed in the heavens after their deaths. In later years, the phrase degenerated to simply "by jiminy" and its meaning had been lost. Now, although few spacemen knew the history of the phrase, they were using it again, correctly.

Other space talk grew out of space itself, and not history. For instance, the worst thing that could happen to a man was to have his helmet broken. Let the transparent globe be shattered and the results were both quick and final. Hence the oft-heard threat, "I'll bust your bubble."

Speaking of bubbles . . . Rip realized suddenly that he and his men would have to live in bubbles and space suits while on the asteroid. None of the minor planets were big enough to have an atmosphere or much gravity.

If only he could get a look into those cases! But the ship was still decelerating and he would have to wait. He put his head against the chair rest and settled down to wait as patiently as he could.

Brennschluss was a long time coming. When the deceleration finally stopped, Rip didn't wait for gravity. He hauled himself out of the chair and the squadroom and went down the corridor hand over hand. He headed straight for where the supplies were stacked, his Planeteers close behind him.

Commander O'Brine arrived at the same time. "We're starting to scan for the asteroid," he greeted Rip. "May be some time before we find it."

"Where are we, sir?" Rip asked.

"Just above the asteroid belt near the outer edge. We're beyond the position where the asteroid was sighted, moving along what the *Altair* figured as its orbit. I'm not stretching space, Foster, when I tell you we're hunting for a needle in a junk pile. This part of space is filled with more objects than you would imagine, and they all register on the rad-screens."

"We'll find it," Rip said confidently.

O'Brine nodded. "Yes. But it probably will take some hunting. Meanwhile, let's get at those cases. The supply clerk is on his way."

The supply clerk arrived, issued tools to the Planeteers, then opened a plastic case attached to one of the boxes and produced lists. As the Planeteers opened and unpacked the crates, Rip and O'Brine inspected and the clerk checked the items off.

The first case produced a complete chemical cutting unit with an assortment of cutting tips and adapters. Rip looked around for the gas cylinders and saw none. "Something's wrong," he objected. "Where's the fuel supply for the torch?"

The supply clerk inspected the lists, shuffled papers, and found the answer.

"The following," he read, "are to be supplied from the *Scorpius* complement. One landing boat, large, model twenty-eight. Eight each, oxygen cutting unit gas bottles. Four each, chemical cutting unit fuel tanks."

"That's that," Rip said, relieved. Apparently he was supposed to do a lot of cutting on the asteroid, probably of the thorium itself. The hot flame of the torch could melt any known substance. The torch itself could melt in unskilled hands.

The next case yielded a set of astrogation instruments carefully cradled in a soft, rubbery plastic. Rip left them in the case and put them to one side. As he did so, Sergeant-major Koa let out a whistle of surprise.

"Lieutenant, look at this!"

Corporal Santos exclaimed, "Well stonker me for a stupid space squid! Do they expect us to find any people on this asteroid?"

The object was a portable rocket launcher designed to fire light attack rockets. It was a standard item of fighting equipment for Planeteers.

"I recognize the shape of those cases over there, now," Koa said. "Ten racks of rockets for the launcher, one rack to a case."

Rip scratched his head. He was as puzzled as Santos. Why supply fighting equipment for a crew on an asteroid that couldn't possibly have any living thing on it?

He left the puzzle for the future and called for more cases. The next two yielded projectile type handguns for ten men, with ammunition, and standard Planeteer space knives. The space knives had hidden blades which were driven forth violently

when the operator pushed a thumb lever, releasing
the gas in a cartridge contained in the handle. The
blades snapped forth with enough force to break a
bubble, or to cut through a space suit. They were
designed for the sole purpose of space hand-to-hand
combat.

The Planeteers looked at each other. What were
they up against, that such equipment was needed
on a barren asteroid?

Private Dowst opened a box that contained a complete tool kit, the tools designed to be handled
by men in space suits. Yards of wire, for several
purposes, were wound on reels. Two hand-driven
dynamos capable of developing great power were
included.

Corporal Pederson found a small case which contained books, the latest astronomical data sheets, and
a space computer and scratch board. These were
obviously for Rip's personal use. He examined them.
There were all the references he would need for
computing orbit, speed, and just about anything
else that might be required. He had to admire the
thoroughness of whoever had written the order. The
unknown Planeteer had assumed that the space
cruiser would not have all the astrophysics references
necessary and had included a copy of each.

Several large cases remained. Koa ripped the side
from one and let out an exclamation. Rip hurried
over and looked in. His stomach did a quick orbital

Great Cosmos! It Was An Atomic Bomb!

reverse. Great Cosmos! The thing was an atomic bomb!

Commander O'Brine leaned over his shoulder and peered at the lettering on the cylinder. "Equivalent ten KT."

In other words, the explosion the harmless-looking cylinder could produce was equivalent to 10,000 tons of TNT, a chemical explosive no longer in actual use but still used for comparison.

Rip asked huskily, "Any more of those things?" The importance of the job was becoming increasingly clear to him. Nuclear explosives were not used without good reason. The fissionable material was too valuable for other purposes.

The sides came off the remaining cases. Some of them held fat tubes of conventional rocket fuel in solid form, the detonators carefully packed separately.

There were three other atomic bombs, making four in all. There were two bombs each of five KT and ten KT.

Commander O'Brine looked at the amazing assortment of stuff. "Does that check, clerk?"

The spaceman nodded. "Yes, sir. I found another notation that says food supplies and personal equipment to be supplied by the *Scorpius.*"

"Well, vack me for a Venusian rabbit!" O'Brine muttered. He tugged at his ear. "You could dump me on that asteroid with this assortment of junk and

I'd spend the rest of my life there. I don't see how you can use this stuff to move an asteroid!"

"Maybe that's why the Federation sent Planeteers," Rip said, and was sorry the moment the words were out.

O'Brine's jaw muscles bulged, but he held his temper. "I'm going to pretend I didn't hear that, Foster. We have to get along until the asteroid is safely in an orbit around earth. After that, I'm going to take a great deal of pleasure in feeding you to the spacefish, piece by piece."

It was Rip's turn to get red. "I'm sorry, Commander. Accept my apologies." He certainly had a lot to learn about space etiquette. Apparently there was a time for spacemen and Planeteers to fight each other, and a time for them to cooperate like friends. He hoped he'd catch on after a while.

"I'm sure you'll be able to figure out what to do with this stuff," O'Brine said. "If you need help, let me know."

And Rip knew his apology was accepted.

The deputy commander arrived, drew O'Brine aside, and whispered in his ear. The commander let out an exclamation and started out of the room. At the door he turned. "Better come along, Foster."

Rip followed as the commander led the way to his own quarters. At the door, two space officers were waiting, their faces grave.

O'Brine motioned them to chairs. "All right. Let's

have it."

The senior space officer held out a sheet of flimsy. It was pale blue, the color used for highly confidential documents. "Sir, this came in Space Council special cipher."

"Read it aloud," O'Brine ordered.

"Yessir. It's addressed to you, this ship. From Planeteer Intelligence, Marsport. 'Consops cruiser departed general direction your area. Agents report crew *Altair* may have leaked data re asteroid. Take appropriate action.' It's signed 'Williams, SOS, Commanding.' "

Rip saw the meaning of the message instantly. The Consolidation of People's Governments of earth, traditional enemies and rivals of the Federation of Free Governments, needed radioactive minerals as badly, or worse, than the Federation. In space it was first come, first take. They had to find the asteroid quickly. It was to prevent Consops from knowing of the asteroid that security measures had been taken. They hadn't worked, because of loose space chatter at Marsport.

O'Brine issued quick orders. "Now, get this. We have to work fast. Accelerate fifty percent, same course. I want two men on each screen. If anything of the right size shows up, decelerate until we can get mass and albedo measurements. Snap to it."

The space officers started out, but O'Brine stopped them. "Use one long-range screen for scanning high space toward Mars. Let me know the minute you get a blip, because it probably will be that Consops cruiser. Have the missile ports cleared for action."

Rip's eyes opened. Clear the missile ports? That meant getting the cruiser in fighting shape, ready for instant action. "You wouldn't fire on that Consops cruiser, would you, sir?"

O'Brine gave him a grim smile. "Certainly not, Foster. It's against orders to start anything with Consops cruisers. You know why. The situation is so tense that a fight between two space ships might plunge earth into war." His smile got even grimmer. "But you never know. The Consops ship might fire first. Or an accident might happen."

The commander leaned forward. "We'll find that asteroid for you, Mr. Planeteer. We'll put you on it and see you on your way. Then we'll ride space along with you, and if any Consops thieves try to take over and collect that thorium for themselves, they'll find Kevin O'Brine waiting. That's a promise, boy."

Rip felt a lot better. He sat back in his chair and regarded the commander with mixed respect and something else. Against his will, he was beginning to like the man. No doubt of it, the *Scorpius* was well named. And the sting in the scorpion's tail was O'Brine himself.

CHAPTER FIVE

THE SMALL GRAY WORLD

Rip rejoined his Planeteers in the supply room and motioned for them to gather around him. "I know why Terra base sent us the fighting equipment," he announced. "They were afraid word of this thorium asteroid would leak out to Consops— and it has. A Connie cruiser blasted off from Marsport and headed this way."

He watched the faces of his men carefully, to see how they would take the news. They merely looked at each other and shrugged. Conflict with Consops was nothing new to them.

"The freighter that found the asteroid landed at Marsport, didn't it?" Koa asked. Getting a nod from Rip, he went on, "Then I know what probably happened. The two things spacemen can't do are breathe high vack and keep their mouths shut. Some of the crew blabbed about the asteroid, probably at the Space Club. That's where they hang out. The Connies hang out there, too. Result, we get a Connie cruiser after the asteroid."

"You hit it," Rip acknowledged.

Corporal Santos shrugged. "If the Connies try to take the asteroid away, they'll have a real warm time.

We have ten racks of rockets, twenty-four to a rack. That's a lot of snapper-boats we can pick off if they try to make a landing."

The Planeteers stopped talking as the voice horn sounded. "Get it! We are going into no-weight. Prepare to stay in no-weight indefinitely. Rotation stops in two minutes."

Rip realized why the order was given. The *Scorpius* could not maneuver while in a gravity spin and O'Brine wanted to be free to take action if necessary.

The voice horn came on again. "Now get it again. The ship may maneuver suddenly. Prepare for acceleration or deceleration without warning. One minute to no-weight."

Rip gave quick orders. "Get lines around the equipment and prepare to haul it. I'll get landing boats assigned and we can load. Then prepare space packs. Lay out suits and bubbles. We want to be ready the moment we get the word."

Lines were taken from a locker and secured to the equipment. As the Planeteers worked, the ship's spinning slowed and stopped. They were in no-weight. Rip grabbed for a hand cord that hung from the wall and hauled himself out into the engine control room. The deputy commander was at his post, waiting tensely for orders. Rip thrust against a bulkhead with one foot and floated to his side. "I need two landing boats, sir," he requested. "One stays on the asteroid with us."

"Take numbers five and six. I'll assign a pilot to bring number five back to the ship after you've landed."

"Thank you." Rip would have been surprised at the deputy's quick assent if Commander O'Brine hadn't shown him that the spacemen were ready to do anything possible to aid the Planeteers. He went back to the supply room and told Koa which boats were to be used, instructed him to get the supplies aboard, then made his way to Commander O'Brine's office.

O'Brine was not in. Rip searched and found him in the astro-plot room, watching a 'scope. Green streaks called "blips" marked the panel, each one indicating an asteroid.

"All too small," O'Brine said. "We've only seen two large ones, and they were too large."

"Space is certainly full of junk," Rip commented. "At least this corner of it is full."

A junior space officer overheard him. "This is nothing. We're on the edge of the asteroid belt. Closer to the middle, there's so much stuff a ship has to crawl through it."

Rip wandered over to the main control desk. A senior space officer was seated before a simple panel on which there were only a dozen small levers, a visiphone, and a radar screen. The screen was circular, with numbers around the rim like those on an earth-clock. In the center of the screen was a tiny

circle. The central circle represented the *Scorpius.*
The rest of the screen was the area dead ahead. Rip
watched and saw several blips on it that indicated
asteroids. They were all small. He watched, interested, as the cruiser overtook them. Once, according
to the screen, the cruiser passed under an asteroid
with a clearance of only a few hundred feet.

"You didn't miss that one by much," Rip told the
space officer.

"Don't have to miss by much," he retorted. "A
few feet are as good as a mile in space. Our blast
might kick them around a little, and maybe there's
a little mutual mass attraction, but we don't worry
about it."

He pointed to a blip that was just swimming into
view, a sharp green point against the screen. "We
do have to worry about that one." He selected a
lever and pulled it toward him.

Rip felt sudden weight against his feet. The green
point on the screen moved downward below center.
The feeling of weight ceased. He knew what had
happened, of course. Around the hull of the ship,
set in evenly spaced lines, were a series of blast holes
through which steam was fired. The steam was produced instantly by running water through the heat
coils of the nuclear engine. By using groups or com-
binations of steam tubes, the control officer could
move the ship in any direction or set it rolling, spin
it end over end or whirl it in an eccentric pattern.

"How do you decide which tubes to use?" **Rip** asked.

"Depends on what's happening. If we were ducking missiles from an enemy, I'd get orders from the commander. But to duck asteroids, there's no problem. I go over them by firing the steam tubes along the bottom of the ship. That way, you feel the acceleration on your feet. If I fired the top tubes the ship would drop out from under those who were standing. They'd all end up on the ceiling."

Rip watched for a while longer, then wandered back to Commander O'Brine. He was getting anxious. At first, the task of capturing an asteroid and moving it back to earth had been rather unreal, like some of the problems he had worked out while training on the space platform. Now he was no longer calm about it. He had faith in the Terra base Planeteer specialists, but they couldn't figure everything out for him. Most of the problems of getting the asteroid back to earth would have to be solved by Lieutenant Richard Ingalls Peter Foster.

A junior space officer suddenly called, "Sir, I have a reading at two seventy degrees, twenty-three degrees eight minutes high."

Commander O'Brine jumped up so fast that the action shot him to the ceiling. He kicked down again and leaned over the officer's 'scope. Rip got there by pulling himself right across the top of the chart table.

The green point of light on the 'scope was bigger

than any other he had seen.

"It's about the right size," O'Brine said. There was excitement in his voice. "Correct course. Let's take a look at it."

All hands gripped something with which to steady themselves as the cruiser spun swiftly onto the new course. The control officer called, "I have it centered, sir. We'll reach it in about an hour at this speed."

"Jack it up," O'Brine ordered. "Heave some neutrons into it. Double speed, then decelerate to reach it in thirty minutes."

The control officer issued orders to the engine control room. In a moment acceleration plucked at them. O'Brine motioned to Rip. "Come on, Foster. Let's see what Analysis makes of this rock."

Rip followed the commander to the deck below where the technical analysts were located. His heart was pounding a little faster than usual, and not from acceleration, either. He found himself wetting his lips frequently and thought, "Get hold of it, boy. You got nothing to worry about but high vacuum."

He didn't really believe it. There would be plenty to worry about. Like detonating nuclear bombs and trying to figure their blast reaction. Like figuring out the course that would take them closest to the sun without pulling them into it. Like a thousand things—all of them up to him.

The chief analyst greeted them. "We got the orders to change course, Commander. That gave us the location of the asteroid. We're already working on it."

"Anything yet?"

"No, sir. We'll have the albedo measurement in a few minutes. It will take longer to figure the mass."

The asteroid's efficiency in reflecting sunlight was its albedo. The efficiency depended on the material of which it was made. The albedo of pure metallic thorium was known. If the asteroid's albedo matched it, that would be one piece of evidence.

In the same way, the mass of thorium was known. The measurements of the asteroid were being taken. They would be compared with a chunk of thorium of the same size. If it worked out, that would be evidence enough.

Commander O'Brine motioned to chairs. "Might as well sit down while we're waiting, Foster." He took one of the chairs and looked closely at Rip. Suddenly he grinned. "I thought Planeteers never got nervous."

"Who's nervous?" Rip retorted, then answered his own question truthfully. "I am. You're right, sir. The closer we get, the more scared I get."

"That's a good sign," O'Brine replied. "It means you'll be careful. Got any real doubts about the job?"

Rip thought it over and didn't think so. "Not any real ones. I think we can do it. But I'm nervous just the same. Great Cosmos, Commander! This is my first assignment, and they give me a whole world to myself and tell me to bring it home. Maybe it isn't a very big world, but that doesn't change things much."

O'Brine chuckled. "I never expected to get an admission like that from a Planeteer."

"And I," Rip retorted, "never expected to make one like that to a spaceman."

The chief analyst returned, a sheet of computations in his hand. "Report, sir. The albedo measurement is correct. Looks like this may be the one."

"How long before we get the measurements and comparisons?"

"Ten minutes, perhaps."

Rip spoke up. "Sir, there's some data I'll need."

"What, Lieutenant?" The chief analyst pulled a notebook from his pocket.

"I'll need all possible data on the asteroid's speed, orbit, and physical measurements. I have to figure a new orbit and what it will take to blast the mass into it."

"We'll get those. The orbit will not be exact, of course. We have only two reference points. But I think we'll come pretty close."

O'Brine nodded. "Do what you can, Chief. And when Foster gets down to doing his calculations, have your men run them through the electronic computer for him."

Rip thanked them both, then stood up. "Sir, I'm

going back to my men. I want to be sure everything is ready. If there's a Connie cruiser headed this way, we don't want to lose any time."

"Good idea. I think we'll dump you on the asteroid, Foster, and then blast off. Not too far, of course. Just enough to lead the Connie away from you if its screen picks us up."

That sounded good to Rip. "We'll be ready when you are, sir."

The chief analyst took less than the estimated ten minutes for his next set of figures. Commander O'Brine called personally while Rip was still searching for the right landing boat ports. The voice horn bellowed, "Get it! Lieutenant Foster. The mass measurements are correct. This is your asteroid. Estimated twelve minutes before we reach it. Your data will be ready by the time you get back here. Show an exhaust!"

Rip found Koa and the men and asked the sergeant-major for a report.

"We're ready, sir," Koa told him. "We can get out in three minutes. It will take us that long to get into space gear. Your stuff is laid out, sir."

"Get me the books and charts from the supplies," Rip directed. "Have Santos bring them to the chief analyst. I'm going back and figure our course. No use doing it the hard way on the asteroid when I can do it in a few minutes here with the ship's computer."

He turned and hurried back, hauling himself along by handholds. The ship had stopped acceleration and was at no-weight again. As he neared the analysis section it went into deceleration, but the pressure was not too bad. He made his way against it easily.

The chief analyst was waiting for him. "We have everything you need, Lieutenant, except the orbital stuff. We'll do the best we can on that and have a good estimate in a few minutes. Meanwhile, you can mark up your figures. Incidentally, what power are you going to use to move the asteroid?"

"Nuclear explosions," Rip said, and saw the chief's eyes pop. He added, "With conventional chemical fuel for corrections."

He felt rising excitement. The whole ship seemed to have come to life. There was excited tension in the computer room when he went in with the chief. Spacemen, all mathematicians, were waiting for him. As the chief led him to a table, they gathered around him.

Rip took command. "Here's what we're after. I need to plot an orbit that will get us out of the asteroid belt without any collisions, take us as close to the sun as possible without having it capture us, and land us in space about ten thousand miles from earth. From then on I'll throw the asteroid into a braking ellipse around the earth and I'll be able to make any small corrections necessary."

He spread out a solar system chart and marked in the positions of the planets as of that moment, using the daily almanac. Then he put down the position of the asteroid, taking it from the paper the chief analyst handed him.

"Will you make assignments, Chief?"

The chief shook his head. "Make them yourself, Lieutenant. We're at your service."

Rip felt a little ashamed of some of the unkind things he had said about spacemen. "Thank you." He pointed to a spaceman. "Will you calculate the inertia of the asteroid, please?" The spaceman hurried off.

"First thing to do is plot the orbit as though there were no other bodies in the system," Rip said. "Where's Santos?"

"Here, sir." The corporal had come in unnoticed with Rip's reference books.

Rip had plotted orbits before, but never one for actual use. His palms were wet as he laid it out, using prepared tables. When he had finished he pointed to a spaceman. "That's it. Will you translate it into analogue figures for the computer, please?" He assigned to others the task of figuring out the effect Mercury, the sun, and earth would have on the orbit, using an assumed speed for the asteroid.

To the chief analyst he gave the job of putting all the data together in proper form for feeding to the electronic brain.

It would have taken all spacemen present about ten days to complete the job by regular methods, but the electronic computer produced the answer in three minutes.

"Thanks a million, Chief," Rip said. "I'll be calling on you again before this is over." He tucked the sheets into his pocket.

"Any time, Lieutenant. We'll keep rechecking the figures as we go along. If there are any corrections, we'll send them to you. That will give you a check on your own figures."

"Don't worry," Rip assured him. "We'll have plenty of corrections."

Deceleration had been dropping steadily. It ceased altogether, leaving them weightless. O'Brine's voice came over the speaker. "Get it! Valve crews take stations at landing boats five and six. The Planeteers will depart in five minutes. Lieutenant Foster will report to central control if he cannot be ready in that time."

Santos grinned at Rip. "Here we go, Lieutenant."

Rip's heart would have dropped into his shoes if there had been any gravity. Only a little excitement showed on his face, though. He waved his thanks at the analysts and grinned back at Santos.

"Show an exhaust, Corporal. High vack is waiting!"

CHAPTER SIX

Rip rechecked his space suit before putting on his helmet. The air seal was intact and his heating and ventilating units worked. He slapped his knee pouches to make sure the space knife was handy to his left hand and the pistol to his right.

Koa was already fully dressed. He handed Rip the shoulder case that contained the plotting board. Santos had taken charge of Rip's astrogation instruments.

A spaceman was waiting with Rip's bubble. At a nod, the spaceman slipped it on his head. Rip reached up and gave it a quarter turn. The locking mechanism clamped into place. He turned his belt ventilator control on full and the space suit puffed out. When it was fully inflated he watched the pressure gauge. It was steady. No leaks in suit or helmet. He let the pressure go down to normal.

Koa's voice buzzed in his ears. "Hear me, sir?"

Rip turned the volume of his communicator down a little and spoke in a normal voice. "I hear you. Am I clear?"

"Yessir. All men dressed and ready."

Rip made a final check. He counted his men, then

74

personally inspected their suits. The boats were
next. They were typical landing craft, shaped like
rectangular boxes. There was no need for streamlining in the vacuum of space. They were not pres-
surized. Only men in space suits rode in the ungainly
boxes.

He checked all blast tubes to make sure they were
clear. There were small single tubes on each side of
the craft. A clogged one could explode and blow the
boat up.

Koa, he knew, had checked everything, but the
final responsibility was his. In space, no officer or
sergeant took anyone's word for anything that might
mean lives. Each checked every detail personally.

Rip looked around and saw the Planeteers watching him. There was approval on the faces behind
the clear helmets, and he knew they were satisfied
with his thoroughness.

At last, certain that everything was in good order,
he said quietly, "Pilots, man your boats."

Dowst got into one and a spaceman into the other.
Dowst's boat would stay with them on the asteroid.
The spaceman would bring the other to the ship.

Commander O'Brine stepped through the valve
into the boat lock. A spaceman handed him a hand
communicator. He spoke into it. Rip couldn't have
heard him through the helmet otherwise. "All set,
Foster?"

"Ready, sir."

"Good. The long-range screen picked up a blip a few minutes ago. It's probably that Connie cruiser."

Rip swallowed. The Planeteers froze, waiting for the commander's next words.

"Our screens are a little better than theirs, so there's a slim chance they haven't picked us up yet. We'll drop you and get out of here. But don't worry. We have your orbit fixed and we'll find you when the screens are clear."

"Suppose they find us while you're gone?" Rip asked.

"It's a chance," O'Brine admitted. "You'll have to take spaceman's luck on that one. But we won't be far away. We'll duck behind Vesta or another of the big asteroids and hide so their screens won't pick up our motion. Every now and then we'll sneak out for a look, if the screen seems clear. If those high-vack vermin do find you, get on the landing boat radio and yell for help. We'll come blasting."

He waved a hand, thumb and forefinger held together in the ancient symbol for "everything right," then ordered, "Get flaming." He stepped through the valve.

"Clear the lock," Rip ordered. "Open outer valve when ready."

He took a quick final look around. The pilots were in the boats. His Planeteers were standing by, safety lines already attached to the boats and their belts. He moved into position and snapped his own

"*Get Flaming, Foster!*"

line to a ring on Dowst's boat. The spacemen vanished through the valve and the massive door slid closed. The overhead lights flicked out. Rip snapped on his belt light and the others followed suit.

In front of the boxlike landing boats a great door slid open and air from the lock rushed out. Rip knew it was only imagination, but he felt for a moment as though the bitter cold of space, near absolute zero, had penetrated his suit. Beyond the lights from their belts he saw stars, and recognized the constellation for which the space cruiser was named. A superstitious spaceman would have taken that as a good sign. Rip admitted that it was nice to see.

"Float 'em," he ordered.

The Planeteers gripped handholds at the entrance with one hand and launching rails on the boats with the other and heaved. The boats slid into space. As the safety lines tightened, the Planeteers were pulled after the boat.

Rip left his feet with a little spring and shot through the door. Directly below him the asteroid gleamed darkly in the light of the tiny sun. His first reaction was, "Great Cosmos! What a little chunk of rock!" But that was because he was used to looking from the space platform at the great curve of Terra or at the big ball of the moon. Actually the asteroid was fair-sized when compared with most of its kind.

The Planeteers hauled themselves into the boats by their safety lines. Rip waited until all were in, then pulled himself along his own line to the black square of the door. Koa was waiting to give him a hand into the craft.

The Planeteers were standing, except for Dowst. Rip had never seen an old-type railroad or he might have likened the landing boat to a railroad box car. It was about the same size and shape, but it had huge "windows" on both sides and in front of the pilot—windows that were not enclosed. The space-suited men needed no protection.

"Blast," Rip ordered.

A pulse of fire spurted from the top of each boat, driving them bottom-first toward the asteroid.

"Land at will," Rip said.

The asteroid loomed large as he looked through an opening. It was rocky, but there were plenty of smooth places.

Dowst picked one. He was an expert pilot and Rip watched him with pleasure. The exhaust from the top lessened and fire spurted soundlessly from the bottom. Dowst balanced the opposite thrusts of the top and bottom blasts with the delicacy of a man threading a needle. In a few moments the boat was hovering a foot above the asteroid. Dowst cut the exhausts and Rip stepped out onto the tiny planet.

The Planeteers knew what to do. Corporal Pederson produced hardened steel spikes with ring tops.

Private Trudeau had a sledge. Driving the first spike would be the hardest, because the action of swinging the hammer would propel the Planeteer like a rocket exhaust. In space, the law that every action has an equal and opposite reaction had to be remembered every moment.

Rip watched, interested in how his men would tackle the problem. He didn't know the answer himself, because he had never driven a spike on an airless, almost gravityless world and no one had ever mentioned it to him.

Pederson searched the gray metal with his torch and found a slender spur of thorium perhaps two feet high a short distance from the boat. "Here's a hold," he said. "Come on, Frenchy. You, too, Bradshaw."

Trudeau, carrying the sledge, walked up to the spur of rock and stood with his heels against it. Pederson sat down on the ground with the spur between his legs. He stretched, hooking his heels around Trudeau's ankles, anchoring him. With his gloves he grabbed the seat of the Frenchman's space suit.

Bradshaw took a spike and held it against the gray metal ground. The Frenchman swung, his hammer noiseless as it drove the tough spike in. A few inches into the metal was enough. Bradshaw took a wrench from his belt, put it on the head of the spike and turned it. Below the surface, teeth on the spike bit into the metal. It would hold.

The rest was easy. The spike was used to anchor Trudeau while he drove another, at his longest reach. Then the second spike became his anchor, and so on, until enough spikes had been set to lace the boat down against any sudden shock.

The boat piloted by the spaceman was tied to the one that would remain and the Planeteers floated its supplies through a window. It took only a few moments, with Planeteers forming a chain from inside the boat to a spot a little distance away. Even the heaviest crates weighed almost nothing. They passed them from one to the other like balloons.

"All clear, sir," Koa called.

Rip stepped inside and made a quick inspection. The box was empty except for the spaceman pilot. He put a hand on the pilot's shoulder. "On your way, Rocky. Thanks."

"You're welcome, sir." The pilot added, "Watch out for high vack."

Rip and Koa stepped out and walked a little distance away. Santos and Pederson cast the landing boat adrift and shoved it away from the anchored boat. In a moment fire spurted from the bottom tube, spreading over the dull metal and licking at the feet of the Planeteers.

Rip watched the boat rise upward to the great, sleek, dark bulk of the *Scorpius*. The landing boat maneuvered into the air lock with brief flares from its exhausts. In a few moments the sparkling blast of auxiliary rocket tubes moved the spaceship away. O'Brine was putting a little distance between his ship and the asteroid before turning on the nuclear drive. The ship decreased in size until Rip saw it only as a dark, oval silhouette against the Milky Way, then the exhaust of the nuclear drive grew into a mighty column of glowing blue and the ship flamed into space.

For a moment Rip had a wild impulse to yell for the ship to come back. He had been in vacuum before, but only as a cadet, with an officer in charge. Now, suddenly, he was the one responsible. The job was his. He stiffened. Planeteer officers didn't worry about things like that. He forced his mind to the job in hand.

The next step was to establish a base. The base would have to be on the dark side of the asteroid, once it was in its new orbit. That meant a temporary base now and a better one later, when they had blasted the little planet onto its new course. He estimated roughly the approximate positions where he would place his charges, using the sun and the star Canopus as visual guides.

"This will do for a temporary base," he announced. "Rig the boat compartment. While two of you are doing that, the rest break out the rocket launcher and rocket racks and assemble the cutting torch. Koa will make assignments."

While the sergeant-major translated Rip's general instructions into specific orders for each man, the young lieutenant walked to the edge of the sun belt. There was no atmosphere, so the edge was a sharp line between dark and light. There wasn't much light, either. They were too far from the sun for that. But as they neared the sun, the darkness would be their protection. They would get so close to Sol that the metal on the sun side would get soft as butter.

He bent close to the uneven surface. It was clean metal, not oxidized at all. The thorium had never been exposed to oxygen. Here and there, pyramids of metal thrust up from the asteroid, sometimes singly, sometimes in clusters. They were metal crystal formations. He guessed that once, long ages ago, the asteroid had been a part of something much bigger, perhaps a planet. One theory said the asteroids were formed when a planet exploded. This asteroid might have been a pocket of pure thorium in the planet.

There would be plenty to do in a short while, but meanwhile he enjoyed the sensation of being on a tiny world in space with only a handful of Planeteers for company. He smiled. "King Foster," he said to himself. "Monarch of a thorium space speck." It was a rather nice feeling, even though he laughed at himself for thinking it. Since he was in command of the detachment, he could in all truth say this was his own personal planet. It would be a good bit of space humor to spring on the folks back on Terra.

"Yep, I was boss of a whole world, once. Made myself king. Emperor of all the metal molecules and king of the thorium spurs. And my subjects obeyed my every command." He added, "Thanks to Planeteer discipline. The detachment commander is boss."

He reminded himself that he'd better stop gathering spacedust and start acting like a detachment commander. He walked back to the landing boat, stepping with care. With such low gravity a false step could send him high above the asteroid. Of course that would not be dangerous, since the space suits were equipped with six small compressed air bottles for emergency propulsion. But it would be embarrassing.

Inside the boat, Dowst and Nunez were setting up the compartment. Sections of the rear wall swung out and locked into place against airtight seals, forming a box at the rear end of the boat. Equipment sealed in the stern next to the rocket tube supplied light, heat, and air. It was a simple but necessary arrangement. Without it, the Planeteers could not have eaten.

There was no air lock for the compartment. The half of the detachment not on duty would walk in, seal it up, turn on the equipment, and wait until the gauges registered sufficient air and heat, then remove their space suits. When it was time to leave again, they would don suits, open the door and walk out, and the next shift would enter and repeat the process. Earlier models had permanent compartments, but they took up too much room in craft designed for carrying as many men and as much equipment as possible. They were strictly work boats, and hard experience had showed the best design.

The rocket launcher was already set up near the boat. It was a simple affair, with four adjustable legs bolted to ground spikes. The legs held a movable cradle in which the rocket racks were placed. High-geared hand controls enabled the gunner to swing the cradle at high speed in any direction except straight down. A simple, illuminated optical sight was all the gunner needed. Since there was no gravity and no atmosphere in space, the missiles flashed out in a straight line, continuing on into infinity if they missed their targets. Proximity fuses made this a remote possibility. If the rocket got anywhere near the target, the shell would explode.

Rip found his astrogation instruments set carefully to one side. He took the data sheets from his case and examined them. Now came the work of finding the exact spots in which to place his atomic charges. Since the computer aboard ship had done all the mathematics necessary, he needed only to take sights to determine the precise positions.

He took a transit-like instrument from the case, pulled out the legs of its self-contained tripod, then carried it to a spot near where he had estimated the first charge would be placed. The instrument was equipped with three movable rings to be set for the celestial equator, for the zero meridian, and for the right ascension of any convenient star. Using a regular level would have been much simpler. The instrument had one, but with so little gravity to activate it, the thing was useless.

The sights were specially designed for use in space and his bubble was no obstacle in taking observations. He merely put the clear plastic against the curved sight and looked into it much as he would have looked through a telescope on earth.

As he did so, a hint of pale pink light caught the corner of his eye. He backed away from the instrument and turned his head quickly, looking at the colorimeter-type radiation detector at the side of his helmet. It was glowing.

An icy chill sent a shiver through him. Great, gorgeous galaxies! He had forgotten . . . had Koa and the others? He turned so fast he lost balance and floated above the surface like a captive balloon. Santos, who had been standing near by to help if requested, hooked a toe on a ground spike, caught him, and set him upright on the ground again.

"Get me the radiation detection instruments," he ordered.

Koa sensed the urgency in his voice and got the instruments himself. Rip switched them on and read the illuminated dial on the alpha counter. Plenty high, as was natural. But no danger there—alpha particles couldn't penetrate the space suits. Then, his hand clammy inside the space glove, he switched on the other meter. The gamma count was far below the alpha, but there were too many of the rays around for comfort. Inside the helmet, his face turned pale.

There was no immediate danger. It would take many days to build up a dose of gamma that could hurt them. But gamma was not the only radiation. They were in space, fully exposed to equally dangerous cosmic radiation.

The Planeteers had gathered while he read the instruments. Now they stood watching him. They knew the significance of what he had found.

"I ought to be busted to recruit," he told them. "I knew this asteroid was thorium, and that thorium is radioactive. If I had used my head, I would have added nuclite shielding to the list of supplies the *Scorpius* provided. We could have had enough of it to protect us while around our base, even if we couldn't be protected while working on the charges. That would at least have kept our dosage down enough for safety."

"No one else thought of it, either, sir," Koa reminded.

"It was my job to think of it, and I didn't. So I've put us in a time squeeze. If the *Scorpius* gets back soon, we can get the shielding before our radiation dosage has built up very high. If the ship doesn't come back, the dosage will mount."

He looked at them grimly. "It won't kill us, and it won't even make us very sick. I'll have the ship take us off before we build up that much dosage."

Santos started. "But, sir! That means . . ."

"I know what it means," Rip stated bitterly. "It means the ship has got to return in time to give us some nuclite shielding, or we'll be the laughingstock of the Special Order Squadrons—the detachment that started a job the spacemen had to finish!"

CHAPTER SEVEN

EARTHBOUND!

There was something else that Rip didn't add, although he knew the Planeteers would realize it in a few minutes. Probably some of them already had thought of it.

To move the asteroid into a new orbit, they were going to fire nuclear bombs. Most of the highly radioactive fission products would be blown into space, but some would be drawn back by the asteroid's slight gravity. The craters would be highly radioactive and some radioactive debris would be scattered around, too. Every particle would add to the problem.

"Is there anything we can do, sir?" Koa asked.

Rip shook his head inside the transparent bubble. "If you have a good luck charm in your pocket, you might talk to it. That's about all."

Nuclear physics had been part of his training. He read the gamma meter again and did some quick mental calculations. They would be exposed to radiation for the entire trip, at a daily dosage of—

Koa interrupted his train of thought. Evidently the sergeant-major had been doing some calculations of his own. "How long will we be on this rock, sir?

You've never told us how long the trip will take."

Rip said quietly, "With luck, it will take us a little more than three weeks."

He could see their faces faintly in the dim sunlight. They were shocked. Space ships blasted through space between the inner planets in a matter of hours. The nuclear drive cruisers, which could approach almost half the speed of light, had brought even distant Pluto within easy reach. The inner planets could be covered in a matter of minutes on a straight speed run, although to take off from one and land on the other meant considerable time used in acceleration and deceleration.

The Planeteers were used to such speed. Hearing that it would take over three weeks to reach earth had jarred them.

"This piece of metal isn't a space ship," Rip reminded them. "At the moment, our speed around the sun is just slightly more than ten miles a second. If we just shifted orbits and kept the same speed, it would take us months to reach Terra. But we'll use two bombs to kick the asteroid into the orbit, then fire one to increase speed. The estimate is that we'll push up to about forty miles a second."

Koa spoke up. "That's not bad when you think that Mercury is the fastest planet and it only makes about thirty miles a second."

"Right," Rip agreed. "And when we really have the sun's gravity pulling us, we'll increase speed.

We'll lose a little after we pass the sun, but by then we'll be almost home."

It was just space luck that Terra was on the other side of the sun from the asteroid's present position. By the time they approached, it would be in a good place, just far enough from the line to the sun to avoid changing course. Of course Rip's planned orbit was not aiming the asteroid at earth, but at where earth would be at the end of the trip.

"That means more than three weeks of radiation, then," Corporal Santos observed. "Can we take it, sir?"

Rip shrugged, but the gesture couldn't be seen inside his space suit. "At the rate we're getting radiation now, plus what I estimate we'll get from the nuclear explosions, we'll get the maximum safety limit in just three weeks. That leaves us no margin, even if we risk getting radiation sickness. So we have to get shielding pretty soon. If we do, we can last the trip."

Private Dominico saluted, clumsy in his space suit. "Sir, I ask permission to speak."

Rip hid a smile at the little Italian's formal manner. In space, formality was forgotten. "What is it, Dominico?"

"Sir, I think we not worry so much about this radiation, eh? You will think of some ways to take care of it, sir. What I want to ask, sir, is when do we let go the bombs? Radiation I do not know much about, but I can set those bombs like you want them."

Rip was touched by the Italian Planeteer's faith in his ability to solve the radiation problem. That was why being an officer in the Special Order Squadrons was so challenging. The men knew the kind of training their officers had and they expected them to come up with technical solutions as the situation required.

"You'll have a chance to set the bombs in just a short while," he said crisply. "Let's get busy. Koa, load all bombs but one ten KT on the landing boat. Stake the rest of the equipment down. While you're doing that, I'll find the spots where we plant the charges. I'll need two men now and more later."

He went back to his instrument, putting the radiation problem out of his mind—a rather hard thing to do with the colorimeter glowing pink next to his shoulder. Koa detailed men to load the nuclear bombs into the landing craft, left Pederson to supervise, and then brought Santos with him to help Rip.

"The bombs are being put on the boat, sir," Koa reported.

"Fine. There isn't too much chance of the blasts setting them off, but we'll take no chances at all. Koa, I'm going to shoot a line straight out toward Alpha Centauri. You walk that way and turn on your belt light. I'll tell you which way to move."

He adjusted his sighting rings while the sergeant-major glided away. Moving around on a no-weight world was more like skating than walking. A regular walk would have lifted Koa into space with every step. Of course the asteroid had some gravity, but it was so slight that it didn't count.

Rip centered the top of the instrument's vertical hair line on Alpha Centauri, then waited until Koa was almost out of sight over the asteroid's horizon, which was only a few hundred yards away.

He turned up the volume on his helmet communicator. "Koa, move about ten feet to your left."

Koa did so. Rip sighted past the vertical hairline at the belt light. "That's a little too far. Take a small step to the right. Good . . . just a few inches more . . . hold it. You're right in position. Stand where you are."

"Yessir."

Rip turned to Santos. "Stand here, Corporal. Take a sight at Koa through the instrument to get your bearings, then hold position."

Santos did so. Now the two lights gave Rip one of the lines he needed. He called for two more men, and Trudeau and Nunez joined him. "Follow me," he directed.

Rip picked up the instrument and carried it to a point 90 degrees from the line represented by Koa and Santos. He put the instrument down and zeroed it on Messier 44, the Beehive star cluster in the constellation Cancer. For the second sighting star he

chose Beta Pyxis as being closest to the line he wanted, made the slight adjustments necessary to set the
line of sight since Pyxis wasn't exactly on it, then
directed Trudeau into position as he had Koa. Nunez
took position behind the instrument and Rip had
the cross-fix he wanted.

He called for Dowst, then carried the instrument
to the center of the cross formed by the four men.
Using the instrument, he rechecked the lines from
the center out. They were within a hair or two of
being exactly on, and a slight error wouldn't hurt
anyway. He knew he would have to correct with
rocket blasts once the asteroid was in the new orbit.

"X marks the spot," he told Dowst. He put his toe
on the place where the cross lines met.

Dowst took a spike from his belt and made an X
in the metal ground.

"All set," Rip announced. "You four men can
move now. Let's have the cutting equipment over
here, Koa."

The Planeteers were all waiting for instructions
now. In a few moments the equipment was ready,
fuel and oxygen bottles attached.

"Who's the champion torchman?" Rip asked.

Koa replied, "Kemp is, sir."

Kemp, one of the two American privates, took the
torch and waited for orders. "We need a hole six feet
across and twenty feet deep," Rip told him. "Go
to it."

"How about direction, sir?" Kemp asked.

"Straight down. We'll take a bearing on an over-head star when you're in a few feet."

Dowst inscribed a circle around the X he had made and stood back. Kemp pushed the striker button and the torch flared. "Watch your eyes," he warned. The Planeteers reached for belt controls and turned the rheostats that darkened the clear bubbles electronically. Kemp adjusted his flame until it was blue-white, a knife of fire brighter by far than the sun.

Koa stepped behind Kemp and leaned against his back, because the flame of the torch was like an exhaust, driving Kemp backward. Kemp bent down and the torch sliced into the metal of the asteroid like a hot knife into ice. The metal splintered a little as the heat raised it instantly from almost absolute zero to many thousands of degrees.

When the circle was completed, Kemp adjusted his torch again and the flame lengthened. He moved inside the circle and cut at an angle toward the perimeter. His control was quick and certain. In a moment he stood aside and Koa lifted out a perfect ring of thorium. It varied from a knife edge on the inner side to 18 inches thick on the outer edge.

In the middle of the circle there was now a cone of metal. Kemp cut around it, the torch angling toward the center. A piece shaped like two cones set base to base came free. Since the metal cooled in the bitter chill of space almost as fast as Kemp could cut it, there was no heat to worry about.

Alternately cutting from the outside and the center of the hole, Kemp worked his way downward until his head was below ground level. Rip called a halt. Kemp gave a little jump and floated straight upward. Koa caught him and swung him to one side. Rip stepped into the hole and Santos gave him a slight push to send him to the bottom. Rip knelt and sighted upward. Kemp had done a good job. The star Rip had chosen as an overhead guide was straight up.

He bounced out of the hole and as Koa caught him he told Kemp to go ahead. "Dominico, here's your chance. Get tools and wire. Find a timer and connect up the ten kiloton bomb. Nunez, bring it here while Dominico gets what he needs."

Kemp was burning his way into the asteroid at a good rate. Every few moments he pushed another circle or spindle of thorium out of the hole. Rip directed some of the men to carry them away, to the other side of the asteroid. He didn't want chunks of thorium flying around from the blast.

The sergeant-major had a sudden thought. He cut off his communicator, motioned to Rip to do the same, then put his helmet against Rip's for direct communication. He didn't want the others to hear what he had to say. His voice came like a roar from the bottom of a well. "Lieutenant, do you suppose there's any chance the blast might break up the asteroid? Maybe split it in two?"

The same thought had occurred to Rip on the *Scorpius*. His calculations had showed that the metal would do little more than compress, except where it melted from the terrific heat of the bomb. That would be only in and around the shaft. He was sure the men at Terra base had figured it out before they decided that A-bombs would be necessary to throw the asteroid into a new orbit. He wasn't worried. Cracks in the asteroid would be dangerous, but he hadn't seen any.

"This rock will take more nuclear blasts than we have," he assured Koa. He turned his communicator back on and went to the edge of the hole for a look at Kemp's progress. He was far down, now. Pederson was holding one end of a measuring tape. The other end was fastened to Kemp's shoulder strap.

The Swedish corporal showed Rip that he had only about eight feet of tape left. Kemp was almost down. Rip called, "Kemp. When you reach bottom, cut toward the center. Leave an inverted cone."

"Got it, sir. Be up in two more cuts."

Dominico had connected cable to the bomb terminals and was attaching a timer to the other end. Without the wooden case, the bomb was like a fat, oversized can. It had been shipped without a combat casing.

"Koa, make a final check. You can untie the land-

ing boat, except for one line. We'll be taking off in
a few minutes."

"Right, sir." Koa glided toward the landing boat,
which was out of sight over the horizon.

It was nearly time. Rip had a moment's misgiving.
Had his figures or his sightings been off? His red hair
prickled at the thought. But the ship's computer had
done the work, and it was not capable of making a
mistake.

Kemp tossed up the last section of thorium and
then came out of the hole himself, carrying his torch.

Rip inspected the hole, saw with satisfaction it
was in almost perfect alignment, and ordered the
bomb placed. He bent over the edge of the hole and
watched Trudeau pay out wire while Dominico
pushed the bomb to the bottom. The Italian made
a last minute check, then called to Rip. "Ready, sir."

He dropped into the hole and inspected the connections himself, then personally pulled the safety
lever. The bomb was armed. When the timer acted,
it would go off.

Back at ground level, he turned up his communicator. "Koa, is everything ready at the boat?"

"Ready, sir."

The Planeteers had already carried away the torch
and its fuel and oxygen supplies. The area was clear
of pieces of thorium.

Rip announced, "We're setting the explosion for
ten minutes." He leaned over the timer, which rested

near the lip of the hole, took the dial control in his glove and turned it to position ten. He held it long enough to glance at his chronometer and say, "Starting now!" Then he let it go.

Wasting no time, but not hurrying, he and Dominico returned to the landing boat. The Planeteers were already aboard, except for Koa, who stood by to cast off the remaining tie line. Rip stepped inside and counted the men. All present. He ordered, "Cast off." As Koa did so and stepped aboard, he added, "Pilot, take off. Straight up."

The landing boat rose from the asteroid. Rip counted the men again, just to be sure. The boat seemed a little crowded, but that was because the rear compartment took up quite a bit of room.

Rip watched his chronometer. They had plenty of time. When the boat reached a point about ten miles above the asteroid, he ordered, "Stern tube." The boat moved at an angle. He let it go until a sight at the stars showed they were about in the right position, 90 degrees from the line of blast and where they would be behind the asteroid as it moved toward the new course.

He looked at his chronometer again. "Two minutes. Line up at the side if you want to watch, but darken your helmets to full protection. This thing will light up like nothing you've ever seen before."

It was a good thing space cruisers depended on their radar and not on sight, he thought. Usually spacemen opened up visual ports only when landing or taking a star sight for an astro-plot. The clear plastic of the domes had to be shielded from chance meteors. Besides, radar screens were more dependable than eyes, even though they could pick up only solid objects. If the Consops cruiser happened to be searching visually, it would see the blast. But the chance had to be taken. It wasn't really much of a chance.

"One minute," he said. He faced the asteroid, then darkened his helmet, counting to himself.

The minute ticked off slowly, though his count was a little fast. When he reached five, brilliant, incandescent light lit up the interior of the boat. Rip saw it even though his helmet was dark. The light faded slowly, and he put his helmet back on full transparent.

A mighty column of fire now reached out from the asteroid into space. Rip held his breath until he saw that the little planet was sheering off its course under the great blast. Then he sighed with relief. All was well so far.

Someone muttered, "By Gemini! I'm glad we're out here instead of down there!"

The column of fire lengthened, thinned out, grew fainter until there was only a glow behind the asteroid. Rip took his astrogation instruments and made a number of sights. They looked good. The first blast had worked about as predicted, although he wouldn't be able to tell how much correction was needed until he had taken star sights over a period of five or six days.

"Let's go home," he ordered.

Back on the asteroid, a pit that glowed with radio-activity marked the site of the first blast. Rip ordered it covered as much as possible with the thorium that had been taken from the hole. While the men worked, he plotted the lines for the second blast, found the spot, and put Kemp back to work on a new hole.

Two hours later the second blast threw fire into space. In another three hours, with the asteroid now speeding on its new course, Rip set off the explosion that blasted straight back and gave extra speed.

Three radioactive craters marked the asteroid. Rip checked the radiation level and didn't like it a bit. He decided to set up the landing boat and their supplies as far away from the craters as possible, which was on the sun side. They could move to the dark side as they approached the orbit of earth. By then the radioactivity from the blasts would have died down considerably.

He was selecting the location for a base when Dowst suddenly called. "Lieutenant! Lieutenant Foster!"

There was urgency in the Planeteer's voice. "What is it, Dowst?"

"Sir, take a look, about two degrees south of

Rigel!"

Rip found the constellation Orion and looked at bright Rigel. For a moment he saw nothing; then, south of the star, he saw a thin, orange line.

Nuclear drive cruisers didn't have exhausts of that color, and there was only one rocket-drive ship around, so far as they knew.

Rip said softly, "Let's get our house in order, gang. Looks like we're going to get a visit from our friends the Connies!"

CHAPTER EIGHT

DUCK—OR DIE!

Sergeant-major Koa's great frame loomed in front of Rip. "Think they've spotted us, sir?"

Rip hated to say it. "Probably. Koa, can you estimate from the exhaust how far away they are?"

"Not very well, Lieutenant. From the position of the streak, I'd say they're decelerating."

The Planeteers looked at Rip. He was in command, and they expected him to do something about the situation. Rip didn't know what to do. The rocket launcher, their only weapon, wasn't designed for fighting spaceships. It was useful against snapper-boats and people, but firing at a cruiser would be like sending mosquitoes to fight elephants.

He sized up their position. For one thing, they were right out in the open, exposed to anything the Connie cruiser might throw at them. If they could get under cover, there might be a chance. It would at least take the Connies a while to find them.

For a moment he thought of hurrying into the landing boat and sending out a call for help to the *Scorpius,* but he thought better of it. They weren't certain that Connie had spotted them. He would wait until there was no doubt. Meanwhile, they had

103

to find cover.

His searching eyes fell on the cutting torch. If they could use that to cut themselves right into the asteroid . . . suddenly he knew how it could be done. On the sun side he remembered a series of high-piled, giant crystals of thorium. They could cut into the side of one of those. And with Kemp's skill, they might be able to do it in time.

He called, "Kemp! Koa, bring the torch and fuel and follow me."

In his haste he took a misstep and flew headlong a few feet above the metal surface. Koa, gliding along behind him, turned him upright again. He saw that the giant Hawaiian was grinning. Rip grinned back. It was the second time he had lost his footing.

They reached the peaks of thorium and Rip looked them over. The tallest was perhaps 40 feet high. It was roughly pyramidal, with a base about 60 feet thick. It would do.

"Kemp." The private hurried to his side. "Take the torch and make us a cave. Make it big enough for all hands and the equipment."

Kemp was a good Planeteer. He didn't stop to ask questions. He said, "I'll make a small entrance and open the cave out inside." He picked up the torch and got busy.

Rip smiled. The Planeteer was right. He should have thought of it himself, but it was good to see increasing proof that his men were smart as well as tough and disciplined.

"Bring up all supplies," he told Koa. "Move the boat over here, too. We won't be able to bury that, but we want it close by." He had an idea for the landing boat. It could maneuver infinitely faster than the big cruiser. They could put the supplies in the cave, then take to the boat, depending on its ability to turn quickly and on Dowst's skill at piloting to play hide and seek. Dowst certainly could keep the asteroid between them and the cruiser.

The plan would fail when the cruiser sent a landing party. They would certainly come in snapper-boats, and the deadly little fighting craft could blast rings around the landing boat. The snapper-boats had gotten their name because fast acceleration and quick changes of position could snap a man right out of his seat, if he forgot to buckle his harness tightly.

The solution would be to keep the landing boat close to the asteroid. At the first sign of a landing party, they would blast in and take to the cave, using the rocket launcher as a defense.

The supplies began to arrive. The Planeteers towed them two crates at a time in a steady line of hurrying men.

Kemp's torch sent an incandescent knife three feet into the metal at each cut. He was rapidly slicing out a cave. He cut the metal out in great triangular bars, angling the torch from first one side, then the other.

Koa came and stood beside Rip. "I haven't seen the Connie's exhaust for a while, sir. Looks like they've stopped decelerating. We can't see them at all."

"Meaning what?" Rip asked. He thought he knew, but he wanted Koa's opinion.

"They're in free fall now, sir. That could mean they're just hunting in the area. Or it could mean that they've stopped somewhere close by. They could be looking us over, for all we know."

Rip surveyed the stars. "If that's so, they're not too close, Koa. Otherwise they'd block out a patch of stars."

"Well, sir—" Koa hesitated. "I mean, if you were looking over this asteroid and you weren't sure whether the enemy had it or not, how close would you get?"

"Probably about one AU," Rip said jokingly. That was one astronomical unit, equal to about 93 million miles, the distance from earth to the sun.

"That would be a good, safe distance, sir," Koa agreed with a grin.

"But let's suppose the Connie isn't as timid as I am," Rip went on. "He might be only a few miles out. The question is, would he wait to get closer before launching his snapper-boats?"

The big Hawaiian answered frankly, "I've never been in a spacegrab like this before. I don't know what the answer is."

"That Connie Cruiser's Not Too Close, Koa."

"We'll soon know," Rip replied grimly. A thought had just struck him. The *Scorpius* had trouble finding the asteroid because it was just one of many sailing along through the belt. But now the asteroid was the only one traveling *across* the belt. It would make an outstanding blip on any radar 'scope. It wasn't possible that the Connie cruiser had missed the blip and its significance.

"The Connie may be looking us over," Rip added, "but I can tell you one thing for sure. He knows we've taken the asteroid." Only human hands could swerve a heavenly body from its orbit.

Koa looked wistfully at the atomic bomb which remained. "If we had a way to throw that thing at them . . ."

"But we haven't. And the thing wouldn't explode anyway. We don't have the outside casing with an exploder mechanism, so it has to be turned on electrically." Rip could see no way to use the atomic bomb against the Connies. It was too big for use against a landing party. Besides, it would put the Planeteers in danger.

"Ever have trouble with the Connies before?" he asked Koa.

"More'n once, sir. Sometimes it seems like I'll never get a job where I don't have to fight Connies."

Rip was trained in science and Planeteer techniques and he didn't pretend to know the ins and outs of interplanetary politics. Just the same, he couldn't help wondering about the strange relationship between the Consolidation of People's Governments and the Federation of Free Nations.

Connies and Feds, mostly Planeteers but sometimes spacemen, were constantly skirmishing. They fought over property, over control of ports on distant planets and moons, and over space salvage. Often there was bloodshed. Sometimes there were pitched battles between groups of platoon size.

But at that point, the struggle ended. The law of the Federation said that no spaceship could fire on a Connie spaceship, or on Connie land bases, except with special permission of the Space Council. The theory was that small struggles between men, or even between small fighting craft like the snapper-boats, was not war. But firing on a spaceship was war, and the first such act could mean starting war throughout the Solar System.

It made a sort of sense to Rip when he thought about it. Little fights here and there were better than a full war among the planets.

Koa suddenly gripped his arm. "Sir! Look up!"

The short hairs on the back of Rip's neck prickled. Far above, blackness blotted out stars in the shape of a spaceship. The Connie had arrived!

Rip ordered urgently, "Kemp! Stop cutting. The rest of you get the stuff under cover. Ram it!" He hurried to lend a hand himself, hustling crates into the cave.

Kemp had made astonishing progress. There was room for the crates, if stacked properly, and for the men besides. Rip supervised the stacking, then the placement of the rocket launcher at the entrance.

"All hands inside the boat," he ordered. "Dowst, be ready to take off at a moment's notice. You'll have to buck this box around like never before." He explained to the pilot his plan to dodge, keeping the asteroid between the boat and the cruiser.

"We'll make it, sir," Dowst said.

"I'm not worried," Rip replied, and wished it were true. He looked up at the Connie again. It was getting larger. The cruiser was within a few miles of the asteroid.

As Rip watched, fire spurted from the cruiser and it moved with gathering speed toward the asteroid's horizon. He watched the exhaust trail, wondering why the Connie had blasted off.

"He has something up his sleeve," Koa muttered. "Wish we knew what."

"Let's take no chances," Rip stated. "Come on."

The men were already in the boat. He and Koa joined them. They stood at a window, watching the Connie's trail.

The trail dwindled. Koa said, "Something's up!" Suddenly new fire shot from one side of the cruiser and it spun. Balancing fire came from the other side, and for an instant the three exhausts formed a cross with the darkness of the Connie's hull in the center.

Then they could see only the exhausts from the sides. The stern flame was out of sight.

"He's made a full turn to come back this way," Rip stated tensely. "Dowst, get ready."

The Connie was perhaps 20 miles away. It grew larger, and the side jets winked out. A few seconds later fire spurted from the nose.

Rip figured rapidly. The cruiser had gone away far enough to make a turn. It had straightened out, heading right for them. Now the nose tube was blasting, slowing the cruiser down.

He sighted, holding out one glove and gauging the Connie's distance above the horizon, and his heart speeded. The Connie was right on the horizon!

"Ram it!" Rip called. "Around the asteroid. Quick!"

Acceleration jammed him back against his men as Dowst blasted. No sooner had he recovered than acceleration in a different direction shoved him up to the ceiling so hard that his bubble rang. He clawed his way to the window as the Connie cruiser flashed by, bathing the asteroid in glowing flame.

There was a chorus of gasps from the men, as they saw the thing Rip had realized a moment before. The Consops cruiser was playing it safe, using its rocket exhaust as a great blowtorch to burn the surface of the asteroid clean!

The sheer inhumanity of the thing made Rip's stomach tighten into a knot. No asking for surrender, no taking of prisoners. Not even a clean fight. The Connie was doing its arguing with fire, knowing that the exhaust would char every man on the asteroid's surface.

The Planeteers watched as the Connie sped away, blasted with its side jets and turned to come back. Dowst tensed over the controls, trying to anticipate the next move. He touched the firing levers delicately, letting out just enough flame to maneuver. He slid the craft over the asteroid's surface to the side away from the Connie, going slowly enough so they could watch the enemy's every move.

"Here he comes," Rip snapped, and braced for acceleration. The landing craft shot to safety as the cruiser's nose jet flamed. Dowst was just in time. Tiny sparks from the edge of the fiery column brushed past the boat.

Rip realized that the Connie couldn't know the Federation men were in a boat, dodging. The cruiser would make about two more runs, just enough to allow for hitting every bit of the asteroid. Then it would assume that anything on it was finished and send a landing party.

"He'll be back," he stated. "About twice more. Three at most." He suddenly remembered the landing boat radio. "Dowst, where is the radio connection?"

The pilot handed him a wire with a jack plug on the end of it. Rip plugged it into his belt. Now his voice would be heard on the *Scorpius.*

"Calling *Scorpius!* Calling *Scorpius!* Foster reporting. We are under attack. Repeat, we are under attack. Over to you."

The answer rang in his helmet. *"Scorpius to Foster. Hold 'em, Planeteers. We're on our way!"*

"Here comes the Connie," Koa yelled.

Rip braced. The landing boat shot forward, then piled the Planeteers in a heap on the bottom as Dowst accelerated upward.

There was a sudden wrenching crash that sent the Planeteers in a jumbled mass into the front of the boat. It whirled crazily, then stopped.

Rip was not hurt. He shoved at someone whose bubble was in his stomach and cleared the way. "Turn on belt lights," he called. "Quick!"

Lights flared on. He searched quickly, swinging his light. The Planeteers were getting to their feet. His light focused on Private Bradshaw and he gasped.

Bradshaw's face was scarlet, and his skin was flecked with drops of blood. His eyes were closed, and bulging terribly.

Rip jumped forward, but big Koa was even faster. The Hawaiian jerked a repair strip from a belt pouch, slapped it on the crack in Bradshaw's bubble.

Rip wasted no time, either. By the time Koa had the strip in place he had pulled the connections from his belt light. He ran the tips of the wires over the edges of the strip. The current sealed the patch in place instantly.

Koa grabbed the atmosphere control on Bradshaw's belt and turned it. The suit puffed up. Rip watched the repair anxiously in the light from Koa's belt. It held.

Rip reconnected his light as he asked swiftly, "Anyone else hurt? Answer by name."

There were quick replies. No one else had been injured.

"Run for the cave," Rip commanded. "Follow Koa. Santos and Pederson drag Bradshaw."

The Englishman's voice sounded bubbly. "I can make it."

"Good for you!" Rip exclaimed. "Call for help if you need it."

Koa was already out of the craft and leading the way. Rip went out through a window and saw the cause of the trouble. Dowst had been a hair too close to the asteroid. A particularly high crystal of thorium had snagged the craft.

Rip looked for the Connie and saw it starting another turn. They had only a moment or two before the next run. "Show an exhaust," he called. The Connie must have blasted the opposite side of the asteroid while they were hung up.

The cave was a quarter of the asteroid away. Rip stayed in the rear, watching for stragglers. But even Bradshaw was moving rapidly. Koa reached the cave well ahead of the rest, reached for a rack of rockets, and slapped it into the launcher.

Rip urged the men on. The Connie was squared off for another run.

They catapulted to safety as the cruiser flamed past, the exhaust splashing over the metal and sending sparks into the cave.

Rip looked out. That, if he had guessed right, was the last run. He watched the Connie's stern jet cut off, saw the nose exhaust as the cruiser decelerated to a fast stop.

"Check your weapons," he ordered.

He pulled his pistol from the knee pocket and checked it carefully. There was a clip in the magazine. Other clips were in his pocket. The clips were loaded with high velocity shells that exploded on contact. One slug could stop a Venusian *krel,* a mammoth beast that had been described as a cross between a sea lion and a cactus plant.

His knife was in place in the other knee pocket.

The Connie cruiser decelerated, went into reverse, and came to a full stop about a mile from the asteroid. The Planeteers saw fire in two places along the hull, marking the exhausts of two small craft.

"Snapper-boats," Koa said tonelessly. "Five men in each, if those are the regular Connie kind."

Rip made a quick decision. With only one launcher they couldn't guard the whole asteroid. "We'll stay under cover, except for Santos and Pederson. You two sneak out. Take advantage of every bit of cover you can find. I don't want you spotted. When a boat lands, report its position. The Connies operate on different communicator frequencies, so they won't overhear. We'll let them think they've burned the asteroid clean."

He paused. "They'll search for a while. Then, when they're pretty well satisfied that all is quiet, we'll show up." Rip grinned at his Planeteers. "We can have a real, old-fashioned surprise party."

Koa slid the safety catch from his pistol. "With fireworks," he added.

CHAPTER NINE

The snapper-boats came out of the darkness of space, leaving a glowing trail of fire. They were not graceful. Rip could see no beauty in their lines, but to his professional eye there was plenty of deadly efficiency.

The Connie fighting craft looked like three globes strung evenly on a steel tube. The middle globe was larger than the end ones, and it was transparent. From it projected the barrels of two kinds of weapons—explosive and ultrasonic. Five men usually rode in the middle ball. One piloted. The other four were gunners.

The end globes were pierced by five large holes. They were blast holes for the rocket exhaust. Unlike the landing boats, each tube did not have its own fuel supply. One fuel tank served each globe. The pilot could direct the exhaust through any tube or combination of tubes he wished, by operating valves that either sealed or opened the vents.

The system gave high maneuverability to the boats. By playing on the controls with the skill of an organist, the pilot could shift direction with dazzling speed.

Snapper-boats used by the Federation operated on the same principle, but they were of American design, and they showed the American's love of clean lines. Federation fighter craft were slim and streamlined, even though the streamlining was of no use whatever in space. With blast holes at each end, they looked like double-ended needles. The pilot's canopy in the center controlled guns that fired through the front only. Rear guns were handled by a gunner, who sat with back to the pilot.

Where Connie snapper-boats carried five men, the Federation boats carried two. The Connies could fire in any direction. The Federation pilots aimed by pointing the snapper-boat itself, as fighter pilots of conventional aircraft had once aimed their guns.

Rip watched the boats approach. He was ready to duck inside if they decided to look the asteroid over before landing. He hoped they wouldn't catch sight of his two scouts. He also hoped his nervousness would vanish when the fight started. He knew what to do, at least in theory. He had gone through combat problems on the moon during training. But this was different. This was real. The lives of his men depended on his being right, and he was afraid of making a wrong decision.

Sergeant-major Koa, an experienced Planeteer with a lot of understanding, came and stood beside him. He said, "Guess I'll never get over being jittery while waiting for the fight to start. I'm sweating so hard my dehumidifier is humming like a Callistan honey lizard. But it doesn't last long once the shooting begins. I get so busy I forget to be jittery."

Before Rip could reply, the snapper-boats flashed over the cave, circled the asteroid once, and landed on the dark side close by the bomb craters.

The first scout reported. "Santos, sir. I'm fifty yards beyond the stakes where we had the first base. The snapper-boats landed between the first two craters. Men coming out of one boat. I count six. Now they're coming out of the other boat, but I can't see very well."

The other scout picked up the report, his Swedish accent thick with excitement. "I can see them, sor! By Cosmos! There be seven in this boat on my side. I am behind a rock forty yards to sunward of the second crater."

Rip turned up the volume of his communicator. "How are they armed? Santos, report."

"One is carrying a pneumatic chattergun. The rest have nothing in their hands."

"Pederson, report."

"No weapons I can see, sor."

Koa looked at Rip. "They must think the asteroid is clean. Otherwise they'd have more than a chattergun in sight. You can bet they have knives and pistols, too."

Rip had been playing with an idea. He tried it on his men. "These Connies would be useful to us alive, if we could capture them."

It was Dowst who caught his meaning first. "You mean as hostages, sir?"

"That's it. If we could capture them, the Connie cruiser would be helpless. We could use the snapper-boat radios to warn the ship that any false move would mean harm to their men."

Koa shook his head doubtfully. "I'm not sure the Connies worry about their men, but it's worth the try. We can capture some of them if they split up to search the asteroid. But we won't be able to sneak up on them all."

"We have an advantage," Rip reminded them. "We've been on the asteroid longer. We know our way around, and we're used to space-walking. They've just come out of deceleration and they won't have their space-legs yet."

Santos reported. "They're breaking up into groups of two. Three are guarding the snapper-boats. One is the man with the chattergun."

"Are their belt lights on?"

"Yes."

"Then keep out of the beams. Don't let them walk into you. Keep low, and keep moving. Stay over on the dark side."

"We'd better get to the dark side ourselves," Koa warned.

He was right, Rip knew. The Connies didn't have far to search before reaching the sun side. "Koa, you take Trudeau and Kemp. I'll take Dowst and Dominico. Nunez and Bradshaw stay here to guard the cave. If they arrive in twos, let them get into the cave before you jump them. Bradshaw, how do you feel?"

"I'm all right, Lieutenant."

Rip admired the Planeteer's nerve. He knew Bradshaw was in pain, because bleeding into high vacuum was always painful. The crack in the Englishman's helmet had let most of the air out, and his own blood pressure had done the rest. He would carry the marks for days. A few more moments and all air and all heat would have been gone, with fatal results. Fortunately, bubbles didn't shatter easily when cracked. To destroy them took a good blow that knocked out a piece.

"All right. Let's travel. Koa, go right. I'll go the other way and we'll work around the asteroid until we meet."

Rip led the way, gliding as rapidly as he could toward the edge of darkness. He called, "Santos. Any coming in the direction of the cave?"

"Two pair. About fifty yards apart. They will be out of my sight in a few seconds."

Which meant they would be within sight of Rip and the others. He knew Koa had heard the message, too. Both groups put on more speed, and reached the safety of darkness. "Get down," Rip ordered. They could still be seen, if silhouetted against the edges of sunlight.

Starlight gave a little light, but it was too faint to
see much. Rip's plan was that the Connies would
supply the light needed for an attack.

In a few seconds, as Santos had predicted, belt
light beams cut sharp paths through the darkness.
Rip sized up the possibilities. There were two teams
of two men each, and they were getting farther apart
with each step. One team was coming almost directly
toward them. The other team was slanting away from
them and would soon be out of sight behind the
thorium crystals in which the cave was located. Fortunately, the Connies were going away from the
cave.

A Connie from the near-by team swung his beam
back and forth, and it cut space over their heads.
Rip saw a few low pyramids of thorium a few rods
away. He directed swiftly, "Dowst, take my boots.
Dominico, take Dowst's boots."

He lay face down on the metal ground until he
felt hands grip his boots, then he asked, "All set?"
Two voices answered. "Ready."

Rip put his gloves on the ground and pulled himself forward and slightly upward. Since there was
very little gravity, the action both lifted and pulled
him. He slid parallel to the surface and a foot above
it, heading for the crystals. Once or twice he reached
down and gave another push. It was like swimming,
except that only the tips of his gloves touched the

ground, and there was no resistance of any kind. He felt Dowst's grip on his boots, but he couldn't feel the weight of his men.

He reached the first crystal and directed, "Get behind these rocks and stay down. Feel your way. Use me for a guide. I'll hold on until you're under cover." He gripped a crystal. "Come on."

Dominico pulled himself along Dowst's prone form, and then along Rip's. When Dominico had reached the shelter of the crystals, Dowst crawled along with Rip's body for his guide, passed over him, and reached cover. Rip followed.

The belt lights of the two Connies were almost abreast of them. Far to their left, Rip saw another pair of lights. That was a pair he hadn't seen before.

"We'll wait until they pass," he told his men. "Then we'll get up and rush them from behind. They can't hear us coming. Dowst, you take the near one. I'll take the far one. Dominico, you help as needed, but concentrate on cutting off their equipment. The first thing we must do is cut their communicators. Otherwise they'll warn the rest. Then turn off their air supplies and collapse their suits."

One thing was in their favor. The space suits worn by the Connies were almost the same as theirs. The controls were of the same kind. The only way to know a Connie was by his bubble, which was a little more tubular than the round bubbles of the Federation.

Rip suddenly realized that he wasn't nervous anymore. He grinned, licking his lips. After all, this was what he had been trained for.

The Connies came abreast and passed. "Let's go," Rip said, and as he rose he heard Koa's voice.

The sergeant-major said, "Kemp, kneel on their right side. Trudeau and I will hit them from the left and tumble them over you. Get their communicators first."

Koa had methods of his own, apparently, and they sounded good.

Rip started slowly. He wanted to get directly behind the Connies. He stayed down low until he was sure they couldn't see him, unless they turned.

Dowst and Dominico were right with him. "Come on," he said, and started gliding after the helmeted figures. He kept his eyes on the one he had selected, and he called on all the myriad stars of space to give him luck. If the men turned, his plan for quick victory would fail.

He sensed his Planeteers beside him as the figures loomed ahead. He gave a final spring that sent him through space with knees bent and outthrust, his hands reaching.

His knees connected solidly with the Connie's thighs and his hands groped around the bulky space suit. He felt a rheostat control and twisted savagely, then groped for the distinctive star-shaped button of the air supply.

Rip Used a Flying Tackle on the Connie

The Connie wrenched violently and threw them both upward. Rip felt the star shape and twisted. If he could only deflate the Connie's suit! But the man was writhing from his grip, clawing for a weapon.

Rip stopped reaching for the deflation valve. He grabbed for his knife, jerked it free, and thrust it against the middle of the Connie's back. Then he clanged his bubble against the man's helmet for direct communication and shouted, "Grab some space, or I'll let vack into you!"

The Connie understood English. Most earthlings did. But even better was his understanding of the pressure on his back. He stopped struggling and his arms shot starward.

Rip breathed freely for the first time since he had leaped, and exultation grew in him. He had his first man! His first hand-to-hand fight had ended in victory so easy that he could hardly believe it.

He took time to look around him and saw that he was a good five feet above the asteroid. Below him, a Connie belt light sent its shaft parallel with the ground, and he knew the second man was down.

The question was, had either of them shouted before their communicators were cut off?

"Dowst," he called urgently. "All okay?"

"No," Dowst said grimly. "We got the Connie, but he got Dominico. Cut his leg with a space knife. I'm putting a patch on it. You okay?"

"Yes. When you can, pull me down."

"Right."

Dominico spoke up. "Don't worry about me, sir. Nothing bad. I don't lose much air."

"Fine, Dominico. Glad it wasn't worse."

But Rip knew it wasn't good, either. A cut with a space knife let air out of the suit and created at least a partial vacuum. If it also cut flesh, the vacuum let the blood pressure force out blood and tissue to turn a minor wound into an ugly one.

They would have to bring this spaceflap with the Connies to a quick end, Rip thought. He had to get his men into air, somehow, to take a look at their wounds. Bradshaw needed attention, and now so did Dominico.

Dowst reached up, took Rip's ankle, and pulled him down. Rip held onto his captive. Then the private bound the Connie's hands, jerked his communicator control completely off, and turned his air back on. Since Rip had been unable to collapse the suit, the Connie was comfortable enough. The reason for collapsing the suit was to deprive the enemy of air instantly, so that he could be tied up while helpless from lack of oxygen. There was enough air in the suit to last for a few minutes.

The Connie on the ground was neatly trussed. Rip's prisoner joined him. Dowst switched off his belt light. "Now what, sir?"

Dominico was standing patiently near by. He said nothing. Rip knew that no more could be done for the Italian at present. "Go back to the cave, Dominico," he ordered.

"I can stay with you, sir."

"No, Dominico. Thanks for the offer, but we'll get along. Go back to the cave."

"Yessir."

Rip was a little worried. He had heard nothing from Koa since that first exchange. He told Dowst as much. Koa himself heard and answered.

"Lieutenant, we're all right. Got two Connies, and I don't think they had a chance to yell. But I'm sorry about one, sir. Kemp had to swing at him and busted his bubble."

"Fatal?"

"No, we got a patch on in time. But worse than Bradshaw."

"Tough." Rip couldn't feel too sympathetic. After all, it was the Connie cruiser's fault Bradshaw had felt high vack. "All right. We have four. That leaves nine."

Santos came on the circuit. "Sir, this is Santos. Only three men are at the snapper-boats. If you can get here without being seen, maybe we could knock them off. The rest wouldn't be much good if we had their boats."

"You're right, Santos," Rip replied instantly. Why hadn't he seen that for himself? He knew how he and Dowst could approach the craters without being spotted, now that they had removed two teams of

Connies. "We're on our way. Koa, make it if you can."

"Yes, sir."

Dominico was already making his way back to the cave. Rip and Dowst started for the horizon at a good walk, not afraid now to use their lights, at least for a few yards. If any of the remaining Connie search teams saw the lights they would think it was two of their own men.

Rip remembered the lay of the ground, and Santos's description of the snapper-boats' position. He circled almost to the horizon, then told Dowst to cut his light. He cut his own. In a moment they topped the horizon, and standing with only helmets visible from the snapper-boats, looked the situation over.

The three Connies were standing between him and the boats. To the left of the boats was the second crater. Rip studied the ground as best he could in the Connie belt lights and decided on a plan of action. Calling to Dowst, he circled again. Presently they were approaching the crater. The Connies were about 25 yards from the crater's opposite rim.

Rip said, "I hate to do this, Dowst, but I can't see any way out. We have to go into the crater."

Dowst merely said, "Yes, sir."

The extra radiation might put both of them well over the safety limits long before earth was reached, and they both knew it. Rip didn't hesitate. He reached the crater's edge and walked right down into it.

They were out of sight of the Connies now. Rip walked up the other side of the crater until his bubble was just below ground level. The chunks of thorium he had ordered thrown in to block some of the radiation made walking a little difficult.

"Santos," he said, "we're in the second crater."

"Sir, I'm beyond the first, between two crystals. Pederson is near you somewhere."

"Good. When I give the word, turn up your helmet light until they can see a pretty good glow. Keep watching them." The bubbles were equipped with lights, but they were seldom used. He outlined his plan swiftly. Both Santos and Dowst acknowledged.

Koa reported in. "We're after two more Connies near the wreck of the landing boat, sir."

"Be careful. Pederson, go help Koa. Nunez, how are things at the cave?"

"Nunez reporting, sir. Two Connies in sight, but they haven't seen us yet."

"Let me know when they spot the cave."

"Yes, sir."

"Santos, go ahead."

For long moments there was silence. Rip felt for a solid foothold, found one, and flexed his knees. He kept his back straight and his eyes on the crater rim. His hands were occupied with two air bottles taken from his belt, and his thumbs were on their valve releases. He waited patiently for word from Santos that his helmet glow had been seen.

Santos yelled, "Now!"

Rip's legs straightened with a mighty thrust. He flashed into space headfirst, at an angle that took him over the crater's rim and 50 feet above the ground. He caught a glimpse of Santos's helmet, glowing like a pink balloon, and of the three Connies facing it, one with gun upraised.

Rip's arms flashed above his head. His thumbs compressed. Air spurted from the two bottles, driving him downward, feet first, directly at the heads of the Connies!

CHAPTER TEN

GET THE SCORPION!

From the corner of his eye Rip saw Dowst's heavy space boots and knew the private was right with him. As they drove down, one of the Connies stepped a little distance away from the others, probably to get a better look at Santos. The Connie sensed something and turned, just as Rip and Dowst flashed downward on his two mates.

Rip's boots caught one Connie where his bubble joined his suit, and the impact drove the man downward to the unyielding surface of the asteroid with a soundless smash. Rip threw up his arms to cushion his helmet as he struck the ground beyond his enemy. He threw the air bottles away. He fought to keep his feet under him and almost succeeded, but his knees hit the ground and pistol and knife bit into them painfully.

Two figures came into his view, locked tightly together, arms flailing. It was Dowst and the second Connie. He got to his feet and was moving to the Planeteer's aid when Santos's voice shrilled in his helmet. "Sir! Look left!"

Rip whirled. The Connie who had stepped aside was advancing, pistol in hand. His light caught Rip full in the face.

The young officer thought quickly. The Connie hadn't fired. Why? Suddenly he had it. The man hadn't fired for fear of hitting his friend, who was battling with Dowst. Rip was in front of them. Quickly he dropped to one knee, reaching for his own pistol. The Connie wouldn't dare fire now. The high velocity slug would go right through him, to explode in one of the struggling figures behind— and the wrong one might get it.

The Connie saw Rip's action and tossed his pistol aside. He, too, knew he couldn't fire. He reached into a knee pouch and drew out his space knife. He leaped for the Planeteer.

Rip pulled frantically at his pistol. It was stuck fast, probably caught in the fabric by his knee landing. The space knife wouldn't be caught. It was smooth, with no projections to catch. He shifted knees and jerked it out.

The Connie's flying body hit him, and a powerful arm circled his waist. Rip thrust upward with his knees, one hand reaching for the Connie's suit valve. But the Connie had one arm free, too. He drove his glove up under Rip's heart. Rip let go of the valve and used his elbow to lever away just as the Connie pressed his knife's release valve. The blade slammed outward, drove into the inside of Rip's right arm just above the elbow.

Pain lanced through him, and he felt the blood

rush to the wound as air poured through the gap in his suit. He gritted his teeth and smashed at the Connie with his own knife. It rammed home and he squeezed the release. The blade connected solidly. He was suddenly free.

He pressed the wounded arm to his side, stopping the outpouring of air. The cut hurt like all the devils of space. With his other hand he increased the air in his suit, then looked swiftly around. The Connie was on his knees, both gloves pressed tightly to his side.

Dowst was just finishing a knot in the safety line that bound a second enemy's hands. The Connie Rip had rocketed down on was still lying where he had fallen. And Corporal Santos, the enemy's pneumatic chattergun at the ready, was standing guard.

Rip turned up the volume in his communicator. He tried to sound calm, but the shakiness of triumph and excitement was in his voice. "All Planeteers. We have the Connie snapper-boats. Koa, bring your men here."

He felt someone working on his arm and turned to see Corporal Pederson, his face one vast grin in the glare from Dowst's belt light. "Koa didn't need me," he said.

Rip grinned back. "Nunez," he called. "How are things at the cave?"

"Sir, this is Nunez. Two Connies were prowling around, but they didn't see the entrance. Then, a minute ago, they turned and hurried away."

Rip considered. "Koa. How many Connies have you?"

· "Four, sir."

With the five he and Dowst had taken, that meant four still at large, and from Nunez's report, some Connie yelling had been going on. The four certainly knew by this time there were Federal men on the asteroid. Unless something were done quickly the four Connies would be shooting at them from the darkness. He ordered, "All Planeteers. Kill your belt lights."

The lights on the Connies they had just taken still glowed. Dowst was putting a patch on the Connie Rip had stabbed. He waited until the private had finished, then said, "Turn out the Connie lights, too."

If he could get in touch with the Connies, he could tell them they were finished. But using the snapper-boat radios was out, because the enemy cruiser would hear. The cruiser couldn't hear the helmet communicators, though, because they carried only a short distance. The cruiser was close enough so that a helmet communicator turned on full volume might barely be heard, although it was unlikely.

He couldn't stick his head in a Connie helmet, but he could talk to a Connie by direct communication and have him give instructions.

There was complete darkness with all belt lights

out, but he groped his way to the Connie Dowst had been patching, felt for his helmet, and put his own against it. He yelled, "Do you hear me?"

"Yes." Then, "Why did you patch me?"

It was a perfect opening. "Because we don't want to kill you. Listen. We have all but four of you. Understand?"

"Yes. What will you do with us?"

"Treat you as prisoners. If you behave. Get on your communicator and tell those four men to surrender. Tell them to come to the boats, with lights on. Tell them we'll give them five minutes. If they don't come, we'll hunt them with rockets."

"They will come," the Connie said. "They don't want to die. I will do it."

Rip kept his helmet against the Connie's, but the man spoke in another language, which Rip identified as the main Consops tongue. When he had finished, Rip told his Planeteers to have weapons ready and to keep lights off. Time enough for light when the Connies were all disarmed.

It didn't take five minutes. The Connie teams came quickly and willingly, and they seemed almost glad to give up their pistols and knives. This was not unusual. Rip had seen many Planeteer reports that spoke of the same thing. Many Connies, it seemed, were glad to get away from the iron Consops rule even if it meant becoming Federation prisoners.

Inside one of the snapper-boats, a light glowed. Rip put his helmet against that of the man who had given the surrender order and demanded, "What's that light?"

"The cruiser wants us."

Rip considered demanding that the Connie answer, then thought better of it. He would do it himself. After all, they had hostages. The cruiser wouldn't take any further action. He climbed into the snapper-boat and hunted for the plug-in terminal. It fitted his own belt jack. He plugged in and said, "Go ahead."

There was an instant of silence, then an accented voice demanded, "Why are you speaking English?"

Rip replied formally, "This is Lieutenant Foster, Federation Special Order Squadrons, in charge on the asteroid. Your landing party is in our hands, as prisoners, two wounded, none dead. If you agree to withdraw, we will send the wounded men back to you in one boat. The rest will remain here as hostages for your good behavior."

"Stand by," the voice said. There was silence for several moments, then a new voice said, "This is the cruiser commander. We make a counter-offer. If you release our men and surrender to them, we will spare the lives of you and your men."

Rip listened incredulously. The commanding officer didn't understand. He, Rip, held the whip hand, because the lives of the Connie prisoners were in his hands. He repeated what he had said before.

"And I repeat," the commander retorted. "Surrender or die. Choose now."

"I refuse," Rip stated flatly. "Try anything and your men will suffer, not us."

"You are mistaken," the harsh voice said. "We will sweep the asteroid clean with our exhaust, but this time we will be more thorough. When we have finished, we will hammer you with guided missiles. Then we will send snapper-boats with rockets to hunt down any who remain. We intend to have that thorium. You had better surrender."

Rip couldn't believe it. The cruiser commander had no hesitation in sacrificing his own men! But it was not a bluff. He knew instinctively that the Connie commander meant it. Instantly he unplugged the radio connection from his belt and spoke urgently. "Koa, get everyone under cover in the cave. Hurry! Collect all the Connies and take them with you."

Then he plugged in again. "Commander, I must have time to think this over."

"You have one minute."

He watched his chronometer, planning the next move. When the minute ended, he asked, "Commander, how do we know you will spare our lives if we surrender?" Through the transparent shell of the snapper-boat he saw lights moving toward the horizon and knew Koa was following orders.

"You don't know," the cruiser answered. "You must take our word for it. But if you surrender, we have no reason to wish you harm."

Rip remained silent. The seconds ticked past until the commander snapped, "Quickly! You have no more time."

"Sir," Rip said plaintively, "two of my men do not wish to surrender."

"Shoot them, fool! Are you in command or not?"

Rip grinned. He made his voice whine. "But sir, it is against the law of the Federation to shoot men without a trial."

The commander lapsed into his own language, caught himself, then barked, "You are no longer under Federation law. You are under the Consolidation of People's Governments. Do you surrender or not? Answer at once, or we take action anyway. Quick!"

Rip knew he could stall no longer. He said coolly, "If you had brains in your head instead of high vacuum, you'd know that Planeteers never surrender. Blast away, you filthy space pirate!"

He jerked the plug loose, hesitated for a second over whether or not to take the snapper-boat, and decided against it. He wasn't familiar with Connie controls and there wasn't time to experiment. He headed for the cave as fast as he could glide.

The Connie cruiser lost no time. Its stern tubes flamed, then its steering tubes. It was going to drive directly at the asteroid without making a long run! Rip estimated quickly and realized that the Connie would get to the asteroid at the same time that he reached the cave—if he made it.

He speeded up as fast as he dared. With little gravity on the asteroid, he couldn't fall, but a false step could lift him into space and make him lose time while he got out an air bottle to propel him down again. The thought gave him an idea. Without slowing he took two bottles from his belt, turned them so the openings were to his rear, and squeezed the release valves.

The Connie was gaining speed, blasting straight toward him. Rip sped forward, and crossed to the sun side, intent on the cave entrance, but no longer sure he would make it. The Connie's nose tube shot a cylinder of flame forward, reaching for the asteroid. He saw the fire lick downward and sweep toward him with appalling speed as he put everything he had in a frantic dive for the cave entrance. The flaming rocket exhaust seemed to snatch at him as a dozen hands pulled him to safety, then beat the sparks from his suit.

He was safe. He leaned against Koa, his heart thumping wildly. For a moment or two he couldn't speak, then he managed, "Thanks."

Koa spoke for the Planeteers. "We're the ones to say thanks, sir. If you hadn't thought of stalling the cruiser, and if you hadn't stayed behind to give us time, we'd have some casualties, and so would the Connies we captured."

"There wasn't anything else I could do," Rip replied. "Come on, Koa. Let's see what the cruiser is doing."

They stepped outside. The metal was already cold again. Things didn't stay hot in the vacuum of space.

They didn't see the Connie until the fire of its exhaust suddenly blasted above the horizon, then they ducked for cover. The cruiser had taken a swing at the other side of the asteroid. They peered out again and saw it making a turn to come back.

"He won't get us," Rip said confidently. "Our tough time will come when he sends a fleet of snapper-boats."

"We'll get a few," Koa replied grimly. "Wait! What's he doing?"

The cruiser had started for the asteroid. Suddenly jets flamed from every quarter of the ship. He was using all steering jets at once! Rip watched, bewildered, as the great ship spun slowly, advanced, then settled to a stop just at the horizon.

"He can't be launching boats already," he said worriedly. "What's he up to?"

They ran forward a short distance until they could see below the cave's horizon level. The cruiser released exhausts from both sides of the ship, the outer ones the slightest bit stronger. Rip exclaimed, "Great Cosmos, he's cuddling right up to the asteroid! Why?"

"Hiding," Koa said. "By Gemini! Come on, sir!"

Rip saw his meaning instantly and they raced to
the side of the asteroid, away from the ship. As they
crossed into the dark half, Rip looked back. He
couldn't see the cruiser from here. But he looked
out into space, across the horizon, and knew that
Koa's guess had been right. The distinctive glow of
a nuclear drive cruiser was clear among the stars.

The *Scorpius* had returned!

"The Connie saw it," Rip said worriedly, "but
didn't blast away. That means he's intending to
ambush the *Scorpius*. Koa, if he does, that means
war."

The big Hawaiian shook his head. "Sir, the Connie has guided missiles with atomic warheads just
like our ship does. If he can launch one from ambush
and hit our ship, that's the end of it. The *Scorpius*
will be nothing but space junk. Commander O'Brine
will never have time to get off a message, because
he'll be dead before he knows there is danger."

The logic of it sent chill fear down Rip's spine.
The Connie could get the *Scorpius* with one nuclear
blast and then clean up the asteroid at leisure. The
Federation would suspect, but it would be unable
to prove anything, because there would be no wit-
nesses. If the Connie took time to tow the remains
of the *Scorpius* deep into the asteroid belt, it likely
would never be found, no matter how the Federation

searched.

They had to warn the ship. But how? Their helmet communicators wouldn't reach it until it was right at the asteroid, and that would be too late. They had no other radio. If only the radios in the snapper-boats were on a Federation frequency . . . hey! They could take one of the boats and intercept the cruiser!

He was hurrying toward them before Koa understood what he was saying. He tried to make his legs go faster, but they were unsteady. He knew he was losing blood. He had lost plenty. He gritted his teeth and kept going.

The snapper-boats seemed miles away to Rip, but he plugged ahead until his belt light picked them up. He took a long look, then turned away, heartsick. The Connie's exhaust had charred them into wreckage.

"Now what?" he asked.

"I don't know, sir," Koa answered somberly.

They went back to the cave, not hurrying because Rip no longer had the strength to hurry. Weakness and a deep desire to sleep almost overcame him, and he knew that he was finished anyway. His wound must be too deep to clot, which meant it would bleed until he bled to death. Whether he warned the *Scorpius* or not, his end was the same.

Back in the cave, he leaned against the wall and asked tiredly, "How is Dominico?"

"I am fine, sir. My wound stopped bleeding."

"How is the Connie I got?"

"Unconscious, sir," Santos replied. "He must be bleeding badly, but we can't tell. The one you landed on is all right now, but he may have a broken rib or two."

Because his voice was weak, Rip had to turn up the volume on his communicator to tell the Planeteers about the *Scorpius*. They were silent when he finished, then Dowst spoke up.

"Looks like they have us, sir. But we'll take plenty of them with us before we're finished."

"That's the spirit," Rip approved. He told them, "I won't last much longer. When I get too weak, Koa will take over. Meanwhile, I want to get outside. Bring the rocket launcher outside, too. Who's the gunner? Santos? Stand by, then. We'll need you in case the Connie decides to send a few snappers before it goes after the *Scorpius*."

The cruiser's glow was plain above the horizon, now. It was so close they could make out its form against the background of stars. O'Brine was decelerating and Rip was certain he was watching his screens for a sign of the enemy. He would see nothing, because the enemy was in the shadow of the asteroid. He would think the coast was clear, and come to a stop near by while he asked why Rip had called for help. Failing to get a reply, since the landing boat was wrecked, he would send a landing party, and the Connie would attack while he was launching boats, off guard.

Rip watched the prediction come true. The nuclear cruiser slowed gradually, its great bulk nearing the asteroid. O'Brine was operating as expected.

Rip was having trouble keeping his vision from blurring. He leaned against the rocket launcher and his glove caressed one of the sharp noses in the rack.

He heard his own voice before the idea had even taken full form. "Santos! Do you hear me? Santos! Get the *Scorpius!* Fire before it comes to a stop. And don't miss!"

Santos started to protest, but Koa bellowed, "Do it. The lieutenant's right. It's the only chance we've got to warn the ship. Get that scorpion, Santos. Dead amidships!"

The Filipino corporal swung into action. His space gloves flew as he cranked the launcher around, turned on the illuminated sight and bent low over it. Rip stood behind the corporal. He saw the cruiser's shape stand out in the glow of the sight, saw the sighting rings move as Santos corrected for its speed.

The corporal fired. Fire flared back past his shoulder. The rocket flashed away, its trail dwindling as it sped toward the great bulk above. It reached brennschluss and there was darkness. Rip held his breath for long seconds, then he gave a weak cry of victory.

A blossom of orange fire marked a perfect hit.

CHAPTER ELEVEN

HARD WORDS FOR O'BRINE

The *Scorpius* could have taken direct hits with little or no major damage from a hundred rockets of the kind Rip had used, but Commander O'Brine took no chances. When the alarm bell signaled that the outer hull had been hit, the commander acted instantly with a bellowed order.

The Planeteers on the asteroid blinked with the speed of the cruiser's getaway. Fire flamed from the stern tubes for an instant and then there was nothing but a fading glow where the *Scorpius* had been.

Rip had a mental image of everything movable in the ship crashing against bulkheads with the terrific acceleration.

And in the same moment, the Consops cruiser reacted. The Connie commander was ready to fire guided missiles, when his target suddenly, mysteriously blasted into space at optimum acceleration. There was only one reason the Connie could imagine: his cruiser had been spotted. The ambush had failed. It was one thing for the Connie to lie in ambush for a single, deadly surprise blast at the Federation cruiser. It was quite another to face the nuclear drive ship with its missile ports cleared for action. The Connie knew he had lost.

Rip and the Planeteers saw the Consops ship suddenly flame away, then turn and dive for low space below the asteroid belt in a direction opposite the one the *Scorpius* had taken. The helmet communicators rang with their cheers.

The young officer clapped Santos on the shoulder and exclaimed weakly, "Good shooting!"

The corporal turned anxiously to Koa. "The lieutenant's pretty weak. Can't we do something?"

"Forget it," Rip said. There was nothing anyone could do. He was trapped inside his space suit. There was nothing anyone could do for his wound until he got into air.

Koa untied his safety line and moved to Rip's side. "Sir, this is dangerous, but there's just as much danger without. I'm going to tie off that arm."

Rip knew what Koa meant. He stood quietly as the big sergeant-major put the line around his arm above the wound, then put his massive strength into the task of pulling the line tight. The heavy fabric of the suit was stiff, and the air pressure gave further resistance that had to be overcome. Rip let most of the air out of the suit, then fought for breath until the pain in his arm told him that Koa had succeeded. He inflated the suit again and thanked the sergeant-major weakly.

The tight line stopped the bleeding, but it also cut off the air circulation. Without the air, the heating system couldn't operate efficiently. It was only a matter of time before the arm froze.

"Stand easy," Rip told his men. "Nothing to do now but wait. The *Scorpius* will be back." He set an example by leaning against the thorium crystal in which the cave was located. It was a natural but meaningless gesture. With no gravity pulling at them they could remain standing indefinitely, sleeping upright.

Rip closed his eyes and relaxed. The pain in his arm was less now, and he knew the cold was setting in. He was getting light-headed, and most of all he wanted to sleep. Well, why not? He slumped a little inside the suit.

He awoke with Koa shaking him violently. Rip stood upright and shook his head to clear his vision. "What is it?"

"Sir, the *Scorpius* has returned."

Rip blinked as he stared out into space to where Koa was pointing. He had trouble focusing his eyes at first, and then he saw the glow of the cruiser.

"Good," he said. "They'll send a landing boat first thing."

"I hope so," Koa replied.

Rip wanted to ask why the big Planeteer doubted, but he was too tired to phrase the question. He contented himself with watching the cruiser.

In a short time the *Scorpius* was balanced with nose tubes counteracting the thrust of stern tubes, ready to flash into space again at a second's notice.

Rip watched, puzzled. The cruiser was miles away. Why didn't it come any closer? Then, suddenly, it erupted a dozen fiery streaks.

"Snapper-boats," someone gasped.

Rip jerked fully awake. In the ruddy glow of the fighting rockets' tubes he had seen that the cruiser's missile ports were yawning wide, ready to spew forth deadly nuclear charges.

The snapper-boats flashed toward the asteroid in a group, sheered off, and broke formation. They came back in pairs, streaking space with the sparks of their exhausts.

"Into the cave," Koa shouted.

The Planeteers obeyed instantly. Koa took Rip's arm, to lead him inside, but the young officer shook him off. "No, Koa. I'll take my chances out here. I want to see what they're up to."

"Great Cosmos, sir! They'll go over this rock like Martian beetles. You'll get it for sure."

"Get inside," Rip ordered. He gathered strength enough to make his voice firm. "I'm staying here until I figure out some way to call them off. We can't just stand here and let them blast us. They're our own men."

"Then I'm staying, too," Koa stated.

A pair of snapper-boats flashed overhead, and vanished below the horizon. Two more swept past from another direction.

Rip watched, curious. What were they up to? Another pair quartered past them at high speed, then two more. The dozen boats seemed to be criss-crossing the asteroid in a definite pattern. Why?

A pair streaked past, and something sped downward from one of them, trailing yellow flame. It exploded in a ball of molten fire that licked across the asteroid in waves. Rip tensed, then saw that the chemical would burn out before it reached them.

"Fire bomb," Koa muttered.

Rip nodded. He had recognized it. The Planeteers were trained in the use of fire bombs, tanks of chemicals that burned even in an airless world. They were equipped with simple jets for use in space.

The snapper-boats drew off, back toward the *Scorpius*. Rip watched, searching for some reason for their actions. Then one of the boats pulled away from the others. It returned to the asteroid with stern jet burning fitfully.

"Is he landing?" Koa asked.

Rip didn't know. The snapper-boat was moving slowly enough to make a landing.

Directly over the asteroid it changed direction, circled, and returned over their heads. Rip could almost have picked it off with a pistol shot. Santos could have blasted it into space dust with one rocket.

The snapper-boat changed direction, and for a fraction of a second stern and side tubes "fought" each other, making the boat yaw wildly, then it

"They're Using Fire Bombs," Muttered Koa

straightened out on a new course.

Koa exclaimed, "That's a drone!"

Rip got it then. A pilotless snapper-boat! That's why its actions were a little uneven. Only one thing could explain its deliberate slowness. It was bait. The *Scorpius* had sent piloted snapper-boats over the asteroid at high speed, criss-crossing in order to cover the thorium world completely, expecting to have the unknown rocketeer fire at them. Then a fire bomb had been dropped as a further means of getting the asteroid to fire. But no rockets had been fired from the asteroid, so the pilot in control of the drone had sent it at low speed, a perfect target.

That meant O'Brine wasn't sure of what was going on. He must have seen the blip on his screen as the Connie cruiser flamed off, Rip reasoned. But the commander probably suspected that the Connies had overcome the Planeteers and were in control of the asteroid. He had sent the snapper-boats to try and draw fire in an attempt to find out more surely whether Planeteers or Connies had the thorium rock.

"The *Scorpius* doesn't know what's going on," Rip told his Planeteers. "O'Brine didn't know the cruiser was waiting to ambush him, so the rocket we fired made him think the Connies had taken us over."

He put himself in O'Brine's place. What would his next step be? The snapper-boats hadn't drawn fire, even when a drone was sent over at low speed.

The next thing would be to send a piloted boat over slowly enough to take a look.

Rip hoped O'Brine would hurry. There was no longer any feeling in his arm below Koa's safety line. That meant the arm had frozen. He had to get medical attention from the *Scorpius* pretty soon.

He gritted his teeth. At least he was no longer losing blood. He wasn't getting any weaker. But every now and then his vision fogged and he had to shake his head to clear it.

The pilotless snapper-boat made another slow run, then put on speed and flashed back to the group of boats near the cruiser. Another boat detached itself from the squadron and moved toward the asteroid.

Rip wished for a communicator powerful enough to reach the *Scorpius*, but knew it was useless to try with his helmet circuit. The carrier waves of the snapper-boats were on the same frequency, and they would smother the faint signal from his bubble.

But the boats might be able to hear if they got close enough! He had a swift memory of the communications circuits. The pilots were plugged into their boat communicators. If a boat got near enough, he could turn up his bubble to full volume and yell. Not only would the boat pilot hear him, but his voice would go through the pilot's circuit and be heard in the ship!

Rip grabbed Koa's arm. "Let's move away from the cave a little farther."

The two of them stepped away from the cave and stood in full view as the snapper-boat moved cautiously down toward the asteroid. Rip planned what he would say. "Commander O'Brine, this is Foster!"

No, that wouldn't do. Connies would know that Kevin O'Brine commanded the *Scorpius,* and if they had taken over the Planeteers on the asteroid, they would also have learned Rip's name. He had to say something that would identify him beyond a doubt.

The snapper-boat was closing in slowly. Rip knew the pilot and gunner must be tense, frightened, ready to blast with their guns at the first wrong move on the asteroid. He groped with his good arm and turned up his helmet communicator to full volume.

The fighting rocket drew closer, cut in its nose tube, and hovered only a few hundred feet above the Planeteers.

Rip summoned enough strength to make his voice sharp and clear. His words sped through space into the bubble of the pilot, echoed in the helmet and were picked up by the pilot's microphone, then hurled through the snapper-boat circuit through space to the control room of the cruiser.

O'Brine stiffened as the speaker threw Rip's voice at him, amplified and hollow-sounding from reverberations in the boat pilot's helmet.

"O'Brine is so ugly he won't look at his face in a clean blast tube! That no-good Irishman wouldn't know what to do with an asteroid if he had one!"

The commander turned purple with rage. He bellowed, "Foster!"

A junior space officer hid a grin and murmured, "Looks like the Planeteers still have the asteroid."

O'Brine bent over the communicator and yelled, "Deputy commander! Launch landing boats. Get those Planeteers and bring them here, under armed guard. Ram it!"

The snapper-boat pilot through whose circuit Rip had yelled turned to look wide-eyed at his gunner. "Did you hear that? Throw a light down on the asteroid. It must have come from there."

The gunner threw a switch and a searchlight port opened in the boat's belly. Its beam searched downward, swept past, then steadied on two space-clad figures.

"It worked," Rip said tiredly. He closed his eyes to guard them against the brilliant glare, then waved his good arm.

Santos called from the cave entrance. "Sir, landing boats are being launched!"

"Bring out the prisoners," Rip ordered. "Line them up. Planeteers fall in behind them."

The landing boats, with snapper-boats in watchful attendance, blasted down to the surface of the asteroid. Spacemen jumped out, awkward at first on the no-weight surface. An officer glided to meet Rip, and he had a pistol in his hand.

"It's all right," Rip told him. "The Connies are

our prisoners. You won't need guns."

The spaceman snapped, "You're under arrest."

Rip stared incredulously. "What for?"

"The commander's orders. Don't give me any arguments. Just get aboard."

"I can't argue with a loaded gun," Rip said wearily. He called to his men. "We're under arrest. I don't know why. Don't try to resist. Do as the spacemen order."

Rip got aboard the nearest landing boat, his head spinning. O'Brine had made a mistake of some kind.

The landing boats, loaded with Planeteers and Connies, lifted from the asteroid to the cruiser. They slid smoothly into the air locks and settled. The massive lock doors slid closed and lights flickered on. . Rip waited, trying to keep consciousness from slipping away.

The lock gauges registered normal air, and the inner valves slid open. Commander O'Brine stepped through, his square jaw outthrust and his face flushed with anger. He bellowed, "Where's Foster?"

His voice was so loud Rip heard him faintly even through the bubble. He stepped out of the landing boat and faced the irate commander.

O'Brine ordered, "Get him out of that suit."

Two spacemen jumped forward. One twisted Rip's bubble free and lifted it off. The heavy air of the ship hit him with physical force.

O'Brine grated, "You're under arrest, Foster, for

firing on the *Scorpius,* for insubordination, and for
conduct unbecoming an officer. Get out of that suit
and get flaming. It's the spacepot for you."

Rip had to grin. He couldn't help it. He started
to reply, but the heavy air of the cruiser, so much
richer and denser than that of the suits, was too
much. He slumped unconscious.

There was no gravity to pull him to the floor, but
the action of his relaxing muscles swung him slowly
until he lay face down in the air a few feet above
the floor.

Commander O'Brine stared for a moment, then
he took the unconscious Planeteer and swung him
upright. His quick eyes took in the patch on the
arm, the safety line tied tightly. He roared, "Quick!
Get him to the wound ward!"

Rip came back to consciousness on the operating
table. The wound in his arm had been neatly re-
paired, and below the wound, where his arm had
frozen, a plastic temperature bag was slowly bring-
ing the cold flesh back to normal. On his other side,
a pulsing pressure pump forced new blood from the
ship's supplies into his veins.

A senior space officer with the golden lancet of
the medical service on his blue tunic bent over him.
"How do you feel?"

Rip's voice surprised him. It was as full and strong
as ever. "I feel wonderful. Can I get up?"

"When we get enough blood into you and your

arm is fully restored."

Commander O'Brine appeared in the door frame. "Can he talk?"

"Yes. He's fine, sir."

O'Brine glared down at Rip. "Can you give me a good reason why I shouldn't have you treated for space madness, then toss you in the spacepot until we reach earth?"

"Best reason in the galaxy," Rip said cheerfully. "But before we talk about it, I want to know how my men are. One got cut and another had his bubble cracked. Also, one of the Connies got badly cut, another had some broken bones, and a third one bled into high vack when Koa cracked his bubble."

The doctor answered Rip's question. "Your men are all right. We put the one with the cracked bubble into high compression for a while, just to relieve his pain a little. The other one didn't bleed much. He's back in the squadroom right now. Two of the prisoners are patched up, but the third one is in the other operating room. I don't know whether we can save him or not. We're trying."

O'Brine nodded. "Thanks, doctor. Now, Foster, start talking. You fired on this ship, scored a hit, and broke the airseal. No casualties, fortunately. But by forcing us to accelerate at optimum speed, you caused so much breakage of ship's stores that we'll have to put into Marsport for new stocks. And on top of all that, you insulted me within the hearing of every man on the ship. I don't mind being insulted by Planeteers. I'm used to it. But when it's done over the ship's communications system, it's bad for discipline."

Rip tried to keep a straight face. He said mildly, "Sir, I'm surprised you even give me a chance to explain."

"I wouldn't have," O'Brine said frankly. "I would have shot off a special message to earth relieving you of command and asking for Discipline Board action. But when I saw those Connie prisoners, I knew there was more to this than just a young space-pup going vack-wacky."

"There was, Commander." Rip recited the events of the past few hours while the Irishman listened with growing amazement. He finished with, "I had to convince you in a hurry that we still held the asteroid, so I used some insulting phrases that would let you know who was talking without any doubt at all. And you did know, didn't you, sir?"

O'Brine flushed. For a long moment his glance locked with Rip's, then he roared with laughter.

Rip grinned his relief. "My apologies, sir."

"Accepted," O'Brine chuckled. "I'm sorry I won't have an excuse for dumping you in the spacepot, Foster. Your explanation is acceptable, but I have a suspicion that you enjoyed calling me names."

"I might have," Rip admitted, "but I wasn't in very good shape. The only thing I could think of was getting into air so I could have my arm treated. Commander, we've moved the asteroid. Now we have to correct course. And we have to get some new equipment, including nuclite shielding. Also, sir, I'd appreciate it if you'd let my men clean up and eat. They haven't been in air since we left the cruiser."

For answer, O'Brine strode to the operating room communicator. "Get it," he called. "The deputy commander will prepare landing boat one and issue new space suits and helmets for all Planeteers with damaged equipment. Put in two rolls of nuclite. Sergeant-major Koa will see that all Planeteers have an opportunity to clean up and eat immediately. The Planeteers will return to the asteroid in one hour."

Rip asked, "Will I be able to go into space by then?"

The doctor replied. "Your arm will be normal in about twenty minutes. It will ache some, but you'll have full use of it. We'll bring you back to the ship in about twenty-four hours for another look at it, just to be sure."

Sixty minutes later, clean, fed, and contented, the Planeteers were again on the thorium planet while the *Scorpius,* riding the same orbit, stood by a few miles out in space.

The asteroid and the great cruiser arched high above the belt of tiny worlds in the orbit Rip had set, traveling together toward distant Mars.

CHAPTER TWELVE

MERCURY TRANSIT

The long hours passed, and only Rip's chronometer told him when the end of a day was reached. The Planeteers alternately worked on the surface and rested in the air of the landing boat compartment while the asteroid sped steadily on its way.

When a series of sightings over several days gave Rip enough exact data to work on, he recalculated the orbit, found the amount that the course had to be corrected, and supervised the cutting of new and smaller holes in the metal.

Tubes of ordinary rocket fuel were placed in these and fired, and the thrust moved the asteroid slightly, just enough to make the corrections Rip needed. It was not necessary to take to the landing boat for these blasts. The Planeteers retired to their cave, which was now lined with nuclite as a protection against radiation.

Rip watched his dosimeter climb steadily as the radiation dosage mounted. Then he took the landing boat to the *Scorpius,* talked the problem over with the ship's medical department and arranged for his men to take injections that would keep them from coming down with radiation sickness.

They left the asteroid belt far behind, and passed within ten thousand miles of Mars. The *Scorpius* sent its entire complement of snapper-boats to the asteroid for protection, in case Consops made another try, then flamed off to Marsport to put in new supplies to replace those damaged when Rip had forced sudden and disastrous acceleration.

The asteroid had reached earth's orbit before the cruiser returned. Of course, earth was on the other side of the sun. Rip ordered a survey and found the best place on the dark side to make a new base. The Planeteers cut out a cave with the torch, lined it with nuclite, and moved in their supplies. It would be their permanent base to the end of the trip.

The sun was very hot now. On the sunny side of the asteroid the temperature had soared far past the boiling point of water. But on the dark side, Rip measured temperatures close to absolute zero.

When the *Scorpius* returned he arranged with Commander O'Brine for the Planeteers to take turns going to the cruiser for showers and decent meals.

The asteroid approached the orbit of Venus, but the bright planet was some distance away, at its greatest elongation to the east of the sun. Mercury, however, loomed larger and larger. They would pass close to the hot planet.

O'Brine recalled Rip to the *Scorpius* and handed him a message.

ASTEROID NOW WITHIN PROTECTION

REACH OF MERCURY AND TERRA BASES.
YOUR ESCORT NO LONGER REQUIRED.
PROCEED IMMEDIATELY TITAN, TAKE ON
CARGO AND PERSONNEL.

The commander sighed. "Looks like I'll never
get to earth long enough to see my family."

Rip sympathized. "Tough, sir. Perhaps the cargo
from Titan will be scheduled for Terra."

"That's what I hope," O'Brine agreed. "Well,
here's where we part. Is there anything you need?"

Rip made a mental check on supplies. He had
more than enough. "The only thing we need is a
long-range communicator, sir. If you're leaving,
we'll have no way to contact the planet bases."

"I'll see that you get one." The Irishman thrust
out his hand. "Stay out of high vack, Foster. Too
bad you didn't join us instead of the Planeteers. I
might have made a decent officer out of you."

Rip grinned. "That's a real compliment, sir. I
might return it by saying I'd be glad to have you
as a Planeteer corporal any time."

O'Brine chuckled. "All right. Let's declare a truce,
Planeteer. We'll meet again. Space isn't very big."

A short time later Rip stood in front of his asteroid base and watched the great cruiser drive into
space. A short distance away a snapper-boat was
lashed to the landing boat. O'Brine had insisted on
leaving it, with a word of warning.

"These Connies are plenty smart. I don't like

leaving you unprotected, even within reach of Mercury and Terra, but orders are orders. Keep the snapper-boat and you'll at least be able to put up a fight if you bump into trouble."

The asteroid sped on its lonely way for two days and then a cruiser came out of space, its nuclear drive glowing. The Planeteers manned the rocket launcher and Rip and Santos stood by the snapper-boat just in case, but the cruiser was the *Sagittarius,* out of Mercury.

Captain Go Sian-tek, a Chinese Planeteer officer, arrived in one of the cruiser's landing boats accompanied by three enlisted Planeteers. They were all from the Special Order Squadron on Mercury.

Captain Go greeted Rip and his men, then handed over a plastic stylus plate ordering Rip to deliver six cubic meters of thorium for use on Mercury. While Koa supervised the cutting of the block, Rip and the captain chatted.

The Mercurian Planeteer base was in the twilight zone, but the Planeteers did all their work on the sun side, using special alloy suits to mine the precious nuclite that only the hot planet provided.

At some time during its first years, Mercury had been so close to the sun that its temperature was driven high enough to permit a subatomic thermonuclear reaction. The reaction had shorn some elements of their electrons and left a thin coating of material composed almost entirely of neutrons. The nuclite was incredibly dense. It could be handled only in low gravity because of its weight. But nothing else provided the shielding against radiation and meteors half so well and it was in great demand for spaceship skins.

"Things aren't so bad," Go told Rip. "The base is comfortable and we only work a two hour shift out of each ten. We've had a plague of silly dillies recently. They got into one man's suit while we were working, but mostly they're just a nuisance."

Rip had heard of the creatures. They were like earth armadillos, except that they were silicon animals and not carbon like those of earth. They were drawn to oxygen like iron to a magnet, and their diamond hard tongues, used for drilling rock in order to get the minerals on which they lived, could drive right through a space suit. Or, if they could work undetected for a short while, they could drill through the shell of a space station.

Scralabus primus was the scientific name of the creature, but the fact that it looked like a silicon armadillo had given it the popular name of "silly dilly." Apart from its desire for oxygen it was harmless.

Koa reported, "Sir, the block of thorium is ready. We've hung it on a line behind the landing boat. The blast won't hurt it, and it's too big to get inside the boat."

"Fine, Koa. Well, Captain, that does it."

The Mercurian Planeteers got into their craft and blasted off, trailing the block of thorium in their exhaust. Rip watched the cruiser take the craft and thorium aboard, then drive toward Mercury, brilliant sunlight reflecting from its sleek sides. The planet was only a short distance away by spaceship. It was the largest thing in space, except for the sun, as seen from the asteroid. To Rip it looked about three times the size of the moon as seen from earth.

Past the orbit of Mercury, the sun side of the asteroid grew dangerously hot for men in space suits. Rip and the Planeteers stayed in the bitter cold of the dark side, which ceased to be entirely dark. Even the temperature rose somewhat. They were close enough to the sun so that the prominences, great flaming tongues of hydrogen that sped many thousands of miles into space, gave them light and enough heat to register on Rip's instruments.

Mercury was left far behind, and earth could not be seen because of the sun. There was nothing to do now but ride out the rest of the trip as comfortably as possible until it was time to throw the asteroid into an ever-tightening series of elliptical orbits around earth, known as braking ellipses. The method would use earth's gravity to slow them down to the proper speed. A single atomic bomb and a half dozen tubes of rocket fuel remained.

Then, as Rip was enjoying the comfort of air during his off-watch hour in the boat compartment, Koa beat an alarm on the door.

Rip and the Planeteers with him hurriedly got into space suits and opened up.

"It's Terra base calling on the communicator, sir," Koa reported. "Urgent message, they said, and they want to talk to you, personally."

Rip hurried to the base cave. The communicator indicator light was glowing red. He plugged in his helmet circuit and said, "This is Lieutenant Foster. Go ahead."

A voice crackled across space from earth. "This is Terra base. Foster, a Consops cruiser has apparently been hiding behind the sun waiting for you. Our screens just picked it up, heading your way. We've sent orders to the *Sagittarius* on Mercury to give you cover, and the *Aquila* has taken off from here. But get this, Foster. The Consops cruiser will reach you first. You have about one hour. Do you understand?"

Rip understood all right. He understood too well. "Got you," he said shortly. "Now what?"

The communicator buzzed. "Take any appropriate action. You're on your own, Foster. Sorry. Sending the cruisers is all we can do. We'll stand by for word from you. If you think of any way we can help, let us know."

Rip asked, "How long before the cruisers arrive?"

"You're too close to us for them to move fast. They'll have to use time accelerating and decelerating. The *Sagittarius* should arrive in something less than two hours and the *Aquila* a few minutes later."

The communicator paused, then continued. "One thing more, Foster. The Connies know how badly we want that asteroid, but they also know we don't want it enough to start a war. Got that?"

"Got it," Rip stated wryly. "I got it good. Thanks for the warning, Terra base. Foster off."

"Terra base off. Stay out of high vack."

Fine advice, if it could be taken. Rip stared up at the brilliant stars, thinking fast. The Connie would have almost an hour's lead on the space patrol cruisers. In that hour, if the Connie were willing to pay the price in blasted snapper-boats, Consops would have the asteroid. And Terra base had made it clear that the space patrol would not try to blast the Connie cruiser and take back the asteroid, because that would mean war.

Added together, the facts said just one thing: they had one hour in which to think of some way to hold off the Connies for an additional hour.

The Planeteers were clustered around him. Rip asked grimly, "Any of you ever study the ancient art of magic?"

The Planeteers remained silent and tense.

"Magic is what we need," Rip told them. "We have to make the whole asteroid disappear, or else we have to conjure up a space cruiser out of the thorium. Otherwise, we have a little more than an hour before we're either prisoners or dead!"

CHAPTER THIRTEEN

PERIL AT PERIHELION

Sergeant-major Koa had made no comment since notifying Rip of the call from Terra base. Now he asked thoughtfully, "Lieutenant, can the Connie launch boats this close to the sun? Won't the sun's pull suck them right in?"

Corporal Pederson scoffed, "Naw, Koa. If sun's gravity be that strong, it pull us in, too."

"Not quite, Pederson," Rip corrected. "Koa is on the right track. The pull of the sun is pretty strong. But I don't think it's strong enough to capture boats."

He had figured the asteroid's orbit to pass as close to the sun as possible while maintaining a margin of safety. He had wanted to use the sun's gravity to pick up speed. His regular star sightings had told him several days before that the sun was dragging them.

But Koa had started a train of ideas running through Rip's head. If they could get close enough to the sun so small boats would be unable to break free of its gravity, the Connie wouldn't dare send a landing force. The powerful engines of a cruiser could break loose from Sol's pull, but not the chem-

169

ical jets of a cruiser's boats.

Rip got his instruments and pulled out a special slide rule designed for use in space. He had Koa stand by with stylus and computation board and take down figures as he called them off.

He recalculated the safety factor he had used when deciding how close to put the asteroid to the sun, then took quick star sights to determine their exact position. They were within a few miles of perihelion, the point at which they would be closest to Sol.

Rip tapped gloved fingers on his helmet absently. If they could blast out of the orbit and drive into the sun . . . he estimated the result. A few miles per second of extra speed would put them so far within the sun's field of gravity that, within an hour or so, small boats would venture into space only at their peril.

He reviewed the equipment. They had tubes of rocket fuel, but the tubes wouldn't give the powerful thrust needed for this job. They had one atomic bomb. One wasn't enough. Not only must they drive toward the sun, they must keep reserve power to blast free again. If only they had a pair of nuclear charges!

He called his Planeteers together and outlined the problem. Perhaps one of them would have an idea. But no useful suggestions were forthcoming until little Dominico spoke up. "Sir, why don't we make two bombs from one?"

"Sir, Why Don't We Make Two Bombs From One?"

"I wish we could," Rip said. "Do you know how, Dominico?"

"No, Lieutenant. If we had parts, I could put bombs together. I can take them apart, but I don't know how to make two out of one." The Italian Planeteer looked accusingly at Rip. "I thought maybe you know, sir."

Rip grunted. If they had parts, he could assemble nuclear bombs, too. Part of his physics training had been concerned with fission and its various applications. But no one had taught him how to make two bombs out of one.

The theory of nuclear explosions was simple enough. Two or more correctly sized pieces of plutonium or uranium isotope, when brought together, formed what was known as a critical mass, which would fission. The fissioning released energy and produced the explosion.

But there was a wide gap between theory and practice. A nuclear bomb was actually pretty complicated. It had to be complicated to keep the pieces of the fissionable material apart until a chemical explosion drove them together fast and hard enough to create a fission explosion. If the pieces weren't brought together rapidly enough, the mass would fission in a slow chain reaction and no explosion would result.

Rip was trained in scientific analysis. He tackled the problem logically, considering the design of a nuclear bomb and the reasons for it.

Atomic bombs had to be carried. That meant an outer casing was necessary. Probably the casing had a lot to do with the design. Suppose no casing were required? What would be needed?

He took the stylus and computation board from Koa and jotted down the parts required. First, two or more pieces of plutonium large enough to form a critical mass. Second, a neutron source—some material with the type of radioactivity that produced neutrons—to start the reaction. Third, some kind of neutron reflector. And fourth, explosive to drive the pieces together.

Did they have all those items? He checked them off. Their single five KT bomb contained at least enough plutonium for two critical masses, if brought together inside a good neutron reflector. Each mass should give about a two kiloton explosion. And they did have a good neutron reflector—nuclite. There wasn't anything better for the purpose.

"What have we got for a neutron source?" he asked aloud. He was really asking himself, but he got a quick answer from Koa.

"Sir, some of the stuff left in the craters from the other explosions gives off neutrons."

"You're right," Rip agreed instantly. A small piece from one of the craters, when combined with half of the neutron source in the bomb, should be enough. As for the explosive, they had exploding heads on their attack rockets.

In other words, he had what he needed—except for a method of putting all the pieces together to create a bomb.

If only they had a tube of some sort that would withstand the chemical explosion—the one that brought the critical mass together!

He told the Planeteers what he had been thinking, then asked, "Any ideas for a tube?"

"How about a tube from the snapper-boat?" Santos suggested.

Rip shook his head. "Not strong enough. They're designed to withstand the slow push of rocket fuel, not the fast rap of an explosion. When I say slow, I mean slow-burning when compared with explosive. Who has another idea?"

Kemp, the expert torchman, said, "Sir, I can burn you a tube into the asteroid."

Rip grabbed the Planeteer so hard they both floated upward. "Kemp, that's wonderful! That's it!" The details took form in his mind even as he called orders. "Dominico, tear down that bomb. Santos, remove two heads from your rockets and wire them to explode on electrical impulse. Kemp, we'll want the tube just a fraction of an inch wider than a rocket head. Get your torch ready."

He took the stylus and began calculating. He talked as he worked, telling the Planeteers exactly what they were up against. "I'm figuring out where to put the charge so it will do the most good, but my data isn't complete. If our homemade bomb goes off, I don't know exactly how much power it will give. If it gives too much, we'll be driven so close to the sun we'll never get free of its gravity."

Bradshaw, the English Planeteer, said mildly, "Don't worry, Lieutenant. We're caught either way. If it isn't the solar frying pan, it's Connie fire."

A chorus of agreement came from the other Planeteers. What a crew! Rip thought. What a great gang of space pirates!

He finished his calculations and found the exact spot where Kemp would cut. A few feet away from the spot was a thick pyramid of thorium. That would do, and they could cut into it horizontally instead of drilling straight down. He pointed to it. "Let's have a hole straight in for six feet. And keep it straight, Kemp. Allow enough room for a lining of nuclite. Koa, pull a sheet of nuclite out of the cave and cut it to size."

Kemp's torch already was slicing into the metal. Rip asked, "Can you weld with that thing, Kemp?"

"Just show me what you want, sir."

"Good." Rip motioned to Trudeau. "Frenchy, we'll need a strong rod at least eight feet long."

The French Planeteer hurried off. Rip consulted his chronometer. Less than ten minutes had passed since the call from Terra base.

He went over his plan again. It had to work! If

it didn't, asteroid and Planeteers would end up as subatomic particles in the sun's photosphere, because he had calculated his blast to drive the asteroid past the limit of safety. It was the only way he could be sure of putting them beyond danger from Connie landing boats or snapper-boats. The Connie would have only one chance—to bring his cruiser down on the asteroid.

If he tried that, Rip thought grimly, he would get a surprise. The second nuclear charge would be set, ready to be fired. The Connie cruiser was so big that no matter how it pulled up to the asteroid, some part of it would be close enough to the charge to be blown into space dust. No cruiser could survive an atomic explosion within five hundred yards, and the Connie would have to get closer to the nuclear charge than that.

Dominico reported that the bomb had been dismantled. Rip went to it and examined the raw plutonium, being careful to keep the pieces widely separated.

This particular bomb design used five pieces of plutonium which were driven together to form a ball. Rip made a quick estimate. Two were enough to form a critical mass. He would use two to blast into the sun and three to blast out again. He would need the extra kick.

There was only one trouble. The pieces were wedge shaped. They would have to be mounted in thorium in order to keep them rigid. Only Kemp could do that. They had no cutting tool but the torch.

Santos appeared, carrying a rocket head under each arm. They had wires wound around them, ready to be attached to an electrical source.

Rip hurried back to where Kemp was at work. The private was using a cutting nozzle that threw an almost invisible flame five feet long. In air, the nozzle wouldn't have worked effectively beyond two feet, but in space it cut right down to the end of the flame. Kemp had his arm inside the hole and was peering past it as he finished the cut.

"Done, sir," he said, and adjusted the flame to a spout of red fire. He thrust the torch into the hole and quickly withdrew it as pieces of thorium flew out. A stream of water hosed into the tube would have washed them out the same way.

Rip took a block of plutonium from Dominico and handed it to Kemp. "Cut a plug and fit this into it. Then cut a second plug for the other piece. They have to match perfectly, and you can't put them together to try out the fit. If you do, we'll have fission right here in the open."

Kemp searched and found a piece he had cut in making the tube. It was perfectly round, ideal for the purpose. He sliced off the inner side where it tapered to a cone, then, working only by eye esti-mate, cut out a hole in which the wedge of fission material would fit. He wasn't off by a thirty-second of an inch. Skillful application of the torch melted the thorium around the wedge and sealed it tightly.

Koa was ready with a sheet of nuclite. Trudeau arrived with a long pole he had made by lashing two crate sticks together.

Rip gave directions as they formed a cylinder of nuclite. Kemp spot-welded it, and they pushed it into the hole, forming a lining.

Nunez found a small piece of material in one of the earlier craters. It would provide some neutrons to start the chain reaction. Rip added it to the front of the plutonium wedge along with a piece of beryllium from the bomb, and Kemp welded it in place.

They put the thorium block which contained the plutonium into the hole, the plutonium facing outward. Trudeau rammed it to the bottom with his pole. The neutron source, the neutron reflector, and one piece of fissionable material were in place.

Kemp sliced another round block of thorium out of a near-by crystal and fitted the second wedge of plutonium into it. At first Rip had worried about the two pieces of plutonium making a good enough contact, but Kemp's skillful hand and precision eye removed that worry.

The torchman finished fitting the plutonium and carried the block to the tube opening. He tried it, removed a slight irregularity with his torch, then said quietly, "Finished, sir."

Rip took over. He slid the thorium-plutonium block into the tube, took a rocket head from Santos and used it to push the block in farther. When the rocket head was about four inches inside the tube, its wires trailing out, Rip called Kemp. At his direction, the torchman sliced a thin slot up the face of the crystal. Rip fitted the wires into it and held them in place with a small wedge of thorium.

Kemp cut a plug, fitted it into the hole, and welded the seams closed. The tube was sealed. When electric current fired the rocket head, the thorium carrying the plutonium wedge would be driven forward to meet the wedge in the back. And, unless Rip had miscalculated the mass of the two pieces, they would have their nuclear blast. Rip surveyed the crystal with some anxiety. It looked right.

Dominico already had rigged the timer from the atomic bomb. He connected the wires, then looked at Rip. "Do I set it, sir?"

"Load the communicator, the extra bomb parts, the rocket launcher and rockets, the cutting equipment, my instruments, and the tubes of fuel," Rip ordered. "Leave everything else in the cave."

The Planeteers ran to obey. Rip waited until the landing boat was nearly loaded, then told Dominico to set the timer for five minutes. He wondered how they would explode the second charge, since they had only the one timer left, then forgot about it. Time enough to worry when faced with the problem.

"I'll take the snapper-boat," he stated. "Santos in the gunner's seat. Koa in charge in the landing boat. Dowst pilot. Let's show an exhaust."

He fitted himself into the tight pilot seat of the snapper-boat while Santos climbed in behind. Then, handling the controls with the skill of long practice, he lifted the tiny fighting rocket above the asteroid and waited for the landing boat. When it joined up, Rip led the way to safety. As he cut his exhaust to wait for the explosion, he sighted past the snapper-boat's nose to the asteroid.

He was moving, and the direction of his move told him the sun was already pulling. Its pull was strong, too. He cut his jets back on, just to hold position, and saw Dowst do the same.

Another few miles toward the sun and the landing boat wouldn't have the power to get away from Sol's gravity. A few miles beyond that, even the powerful little snapper-boat would be caught.

Below, the timer reached zero. A mighty fan of fire shot into space. The asteroid shuddered from the blast, then swerved gradually, picking up speed as well as new direction.

Rip swallowed hard. Now they were committed. They would reach a new perihelion far beyond the limits of safety. P for perihelion and P for peril. In this case, they were the same thing!

CHAPTER FOURTEEN

BETWEEN TWO FIRES

Back on the asteroid, the Planeteers started laying the second atomic charge. Rip selected the spot, found a near-by crystal that would serve to house the bomb, and Kemp started cutting.

The Planeteers knew what to do now, and the work went rapidly. Rip kept an eye on his chronometer. According to the message from Terra base, he had about fifteen minutes before the Consops cruiser arrived.

"We have one advantage we didn't have back in the asteroid belt," he remarked to Koa. "Back there they could have landed anywhere on the rock. Now they have to stick to the dark side. Snapper-boats could last on the sun side, but men in ordinary space suits couldn't."

"That's good," Koa agreed. "We have only one side to defend. Why don't we put the rocket launcher right in the middle of the dark side?"

"Go ahead. And have all men check their pistols and knives. We don't know what's likely to happen when that Connie flames in."

Rip walked over to the communicator and plugged his suit into the circuit. "This is the asteroid calling

Terra base. Over."

"This is Terra base. Go ahead, Foster. How are you doing?"

"If you need anything cooked, send it to us," Rip replied. "We have heat enough to cook anything, including tungsten alloy." He explained briefly what action they had taken.

A new voice came on the communicator. "Foster, this is Colonel Stevens."

Rip responded swiftly, "Yes, sir!" Stevens was the top Planeteer, commanding officer of all the Special Order Squadrons.

"We've piped this circuit into every channel in the system," the colonel said. "Every Planeteer in the Squadrons is listening, and rooting for you. Is there anything we can do?"

"Yes, sir," Rip replied. "Do you know if Terra base has plotted our course this far?"

There was a brief silence, then the colonel answered, "Yes, Foster. We have a complete track from the time you started showing on the Terra screens, about halfway between the orbits of Mars and earth."

"Did you just get our change of direction?"

"Yes. We're following you on the screens."

"Then, sir, I'd appreciate it if you'd put the calculators to work and make a time-distance plot for the next few hours. The blast we're saving to push back to safety is about three kilotons. Let us know the last moment when we can fire and still get free of Sol's gravity."

"You'll have it within fifteen minutes. Anything else, Foster?"

"Nothing else I can think of, sir."

"Then good luck. We'll be standing by."

"Yes, sir. Foster off."

Rip disconnected and turned up his helmet communicator, repeating the conversation to his men. Koa came and stood beside him. "Lieutenant, how do we set off this next charge?"

There was only one way. When the time came to blast, they would be too close to the sun to take to the boats. The blast had to be set off from the asteroid.

"We'll get underground as far away from the bomb as we can," Rip said. He surveyed the dark side, which was rapidly growing less dark. "I think the second crater will do. Kemp can square it off on the side toward the blast to give us a vertical wall to hide behind."

Koa looked doubtful. "Plenty of radiation left in those holes, sir."

Rip grinned mirthlessly. "Radiation is the least of our problems. I'd rather get an overdose of gamma than get blasted into space."

A yell rang in his helmet. "Here comes the Connie!"

Rip looked up, startled. The Consops cruiser passed directly overhead, about ten miles away. It was decelerating rapidly. Rip wondered why they hadn't spotted it earlier and realized the Connie had come from the direction of the hot side.

The enemy cruiser was probably the same one that had attacked them before. He must have lain in wait for days, keeping between the sun and Terra. That way, the screens wouldn't pick him up, since only a few observatories scanned the sun regularly. To the observatories, the cruiser would have been only a tiny speck, too small to be noticed. Or if they had noticed it, the astronomers probably decided it was just a very tiny sunspot.

The Planeteers worked with increased speed. Kemp welded the final plug into place, then hurried to the crater from which they would set off the charge. Dominico and Dowst connected the wires from the rocket head to a reel of wire and rolled it toward the crater. Nunez got a hand-driven dynamo from the supplies and tested it for use in setting off the charge. Santos stood by the rocket launcher, with Pederson ready to put another rack of rockets into the device when necessary.

Rip and Koa watched the Connie cruiser. It decelerated to a stop for a brief second, then started moving again, with no jets showing.

"That's the sun pulling," Rip said exultantly. "They'll have to keep blasting to maintain position."

The Consops commander didn't wait to trim ship against the sun's drag. His air locks opened, clearly visible to Rip and Koa because that side of the cruiser was brilliant with sunlight. Ten snapper-boats sped forth. Rip was certain now that this was the enemy cruiser they had fought off back in the asteroid belt. Two Connie snapper-boats had been destroyed in that clash, which explained why the commander was sending out only ten boats, instead of the full quota of twelve.

The squadron instantly formed a V, like a strange space letter made up of globes. The sun's gravity pulled at them, dragging them off course. Rip watched as flames poured from their stern tubes. They were firing full speed ahead, but the drag of the sun distorted their line of flight into a great arc.

Rip saw the strategy instantly. The Connie commander knew the situation exactly, and he was staking everything in one great gamble, sending his snapper-boats to land on the asteroid—to crash land if necessary.

The asteroid was so close to the sun that even the powerful fighting rockets would use most of their fuel in simply combatting its gravity.

"All hands stand by to repel Connies," Rip shouted, and drew his pistol. He looked into the magazine, saw that he had a full clip, and then charged the weapon.

Santos was crouched over the rocket launcher, his space gloves working rapidly as he kept the rockets pointed at the enemy.

Rip called, "Santos, fire at will."

The Planeteers formed a skirmish line which pivoted on the launcher. Only Kemp remained at work. His torch flared, slicing through the thorium as he prepared their firing position.

The atomic charge was ready. The wires had been laid up to the rim of the crater in which Kemp worked, and the dynamo was attached.

Rip was everywhere, checking on the launcher, on Kemp, on the pistols of his men. And Santos, hunched over his illuminated sight, watched the Connie snapper-boats draw near.

"Here we go," the Filipino corporal muttered. He pressed the trigger.

The first rocket sped outward in a sweeping curve, and for a moment Rip opened his mouth to yell at Santos. The sun's gravity affected the attack rockets, too! Then he saw that the corporal had allowed for the sun's pull.

The rocket curved into the squadron of oncoming boats and they all tried to dodge at once. Two of them met in a sideways crash, then a third staggered as its stern globe flared and exploded. Santos had scored a hit!

Rip called, "Good shooting!"

The corporal's reply was rueful, "Sir, that wasn't the one I aimed at. The sun's pull is worse than I figured."

The damaged snapper-boat instantly blasted from

its nose tubes, decelerated and went into reverse, flipping through space crabwise as it tried to regain the safety of the cruiser. The two boats that had crashed while trying to dodge were blasting in great spurts of flame, following the example of their damaged companion.

"Seven left," Rip called, and another rocket flashed on its way. He followed its trail as it curved away from the asteroid and into the squadron. Its proximity fuse detonated in the exhaust of a Connie boat, blowing the tube out of position. The boat yawed wildly, cut its stern tubes, and blasted to a stop from the bow tube. Then it, too, started backward toward the cruiser.

Six left!

Flame blossomed a few yards from Rip. He was picked up bodily and flung into space, whirling end over end. Koa's voice rang in his helmet.

"Watch it! They're firing back!"

Rip tugged frantically at an air bottle in his belt. He pulled it out and used it to whirl him upright again, then its air blast drove him back to the surface of the asteroid. Sweat poured from his forehead and the suit ventilator whined as it worked to pick up the extra moisture. Great Cosmos! That was close.

Koa called, "All right, sir?"

"Fine."

Santos fired again, twice, in rapid succession. The

Connie snapper-boats scattered as the proximity
fuses produced flowers of fire among them. Two
near misses, but they threw the enemy off course.
Rip watched tensely as the boats fought to regain
their course. He knew asteroid, cruiser, and boats
were speeding toward the sun at close to 50 miles
a second, and the drag was getting terrific. The Connies knew it too.

There was an exultant yell from the Planeteers
as two of the boats gave up and turned back, using
full power to regain the safety of the mother ship.

Four left, and they were getting close!

Santos scored a direct hit on the nose of the nearest one, but its momentum drove it within a few
yards of the asteroid. Five space-suited figures erupted from it, holding hand propulsion units, tubes of
rocket fuel used for hand combat in empty space.

The Connies lit off their propulsion tubes and
drove feet first for the asteroid. The Planeteers estimated where the enemy would land, and were there
waiting with pointed handguns. The Connies had
their hands over their heads, holding the propulsion
tubes. They took one look at the gleaming Planeteer
guns and their hands stayed upright.

The Planeteers lashed the Connies' hands behind
them with their own safety lines and, at Rip's orders,
dumped all but one of them into the crater where
Kemp was just finishing.

Three snapper-boats remained. Rip watched, holding tightly to the arm of the Connie he had kept at his side. The man wore the insignia of an officer.

The remaining snapper-boats were going to make it. Santos threw rockets among them and scored hits, but the boats kept coming. The Connies were too far away from the cruiser to return, and they knew it. Getting to the asteroid was their only chance.

Rip called, "Santos. Cease fire. Set the launcher for ground level. Let them land, but don't fire until I give the word." He hoped his plan would work. Experience back in the asteroid belt had taught him something about Connies.

He put his helmet against his prisoner's for direct communication. "You speak English?"

The man shouted back, "Yes."

"Good. We're going to let your friends land. As soon as they do, I want you to yell to them. Say we have assault rockets trained on them. Tell them to surrender or they'll be killed in their tracks. Got that?"

The Connie replied, "Suppose I refuse?"

Rip put his space knife against the man's stomach. "Then we'll get them with rockets. But you won't care because you won't know it."

The truth was, Santos couldn't hope to get them all with his rockets. They might overcome the Connies in hand-to-hand fighting, but there would be a cost to pay in Planeteer casualties. Rip hoped the Connie wouldn't call his bluff, because that's all it was. He couldn't use a space knife on an unarmed prisoner.

The Connie didn't know that. In Rip's place he would have no compunctions about using the knife, so instead of calling Rip's bluff he agreed.

The snapper-boats blew their front tubes, decelerating, and squashed down to the asteroid in a roar of exhaust flames, sending the Planeteers running out of the way. Rip thrust harder with his space knife and yelled, "Tell them!"

The Connie officer nodded. "Turn up my communicator."

Rip turned it on full, and the Connie barked quick instructions. The exhausts died and five men filed out of each boat with hands held high. Rip blew a drop of perspiration from the tip of his nose. Empty space! It was a good thing Connie morale was bad. The enemy's willingness to surrender had saved them a costly fight.

The Planeteers rounded up the prisoners and secured them while Rip took an anxious look at the communicator. It was about time he heard from Terra base.

The light was glowing. For all he knew, it might have been glowing for many minutes. He plugged into the circuit.

"This is Foster on the asteroid."

"Terra base to Foster. Listen, you will reach optimum position on the time-distance curve at twenty-three-oh-six. Repeat back, twenty-three-oh-six."

"Got it. We will reach optimum position at twenty-three-oh-six." He looked at his chronometer and his pulse stopped. It was 2258! They had just eight minutes before the sun caught them forever, atomic blast or no!

And the Connie cruiser was still overhead, with no friendly cruisers in sight. He looked up, white-faced. Not only was the Connie still there, but its main air lock was sliding open to disclose a new danger.

In the opening, ready to launch, an assault boat waited. The assault boats were something only the Connies used. They were about four times the size of a snapper-boat, less maneuverable but more powerful. They carried 20 men and a pair of guided missiles with atomic warheads!

CHAPTER FIFTEEN

THE ROCKETEERS

Rip ran for the snapper-boat, feet moving as rapidly as lack of gravity would permit. He called instructions. "Santos! Turn the launcher over to Pederson and come with me. Koa, take over. Start throwing rockets at that boat and don't stop until you run out of ammunition."

He reached the snapper-boat and squeezed in, Santos close behind him. As he strapped himself into the seat he called, "Koa! Get this, and get it straight. At twenty-three-oh-five, fire the bomb. Fire it whether I'm back or not. Got that?"

Koa replied, "Got it, sir."

That would give the Planeteers a minute's leeway. Not much of a safety margin, especially when he wasn't sure how much power the improvised atomic charge would produce.

He plugged into the snapper-boat's communicator and called, "Ready, Santos?"

"Ready, Lieutenant."

He braced himself against acceleration and flipped the speed control to full power. The fighting rocket rammed out from the asteroid, snapping him back against the seat. He made a quick check. Gunsight on, fuel tanks almost full, propulsion tubes racked handy to his hand, space patches ready to be grabbed and slapped on in case an enemy shot holed helmet or suit.

They drove toward the enemy cruiser at top speed, swerving in a great arc as the sun pulled at them. The enemy's big boat was out of the ship, its jets firing as it started for the asteroid.

Rip leaned over his illuminated gunsight. The boat showed up clearly, the rings of the sight framing it. He estimated distance and the pull of the sun, then squeezed the trigger on the speed control handle. The cannon in the nose spat flame. He watched tensely and saw the charge explode on the hull of the Connie cruiser. He had underestimated the sun's drag. He compensated and tried again.

He missed. Now that he was closer and the charge had less distance to travel, he had overestimated the sun's effect. He gritted his teeth. The next shot would be at close range.

The fighting rocket closed space, and the landing boat loomed large in the sight. He fired again and the shot blew metal loose from the top of the boat's hull. A hit, but not good enough. He leaned over the sight to fire again, but before he had sighted an explosion blew the landing boat completely around.

Koa and Pederson had scored a hit from the asteroid!

The big boat fired its side jets and spun around

on course again. Flame bloomed from its side as Connie gunners tried to get the range on the snapper-boat.

Rip was within reach now. He fired at point-blank range and flashed over the boat as its front end exploded. Santos, firing from the rear, hit it again as the snapper-boat passed.

Rip threw the rocket into a turn that rammed him against the top of his harness. He steadied on a line with the crippled Connie craft. It was hard hit. The bow jets flickered fitfully, and the stern tubes were dead. He sighted, fired. A charge hit the boat aft and blew its stern tubes off completely.

And at the same moment, a Connie gunner got a perfect bead on the snapper-boat.

Space blew up in Rip's face. The snapper-boat slewed wildly as the Connie shot took effect. Rip worked his controls frantically, trying to straighten the rocket out more by instinct than anything else.

His eyes recovered from the blinding flash and he gulped as he saw the raw, twisted metal where the boat's nose had been. He managed to correct the boat's twisting by using the stern tubes, but he was no longer in full control.

For a moment panic gripped him. Without full control he couldn't get back to the asteroid! Then he forced himself to steady down. He sized up the situation. They were still underway, the stern tubes pushing, but their trajectory would take them right under the crippled Connie boat. The sun was blazing into the fighting rocket with such intensity that he had trouble seeing.

There was nothing he could do but pass close to the Connie. The enemy gunners would fire, but he had to take his chances. He looked down at the asteroid and saw an orange trail as Koa launched another rocket.

The shot from the asteroid ticked the bottom of the Connie boat and exploded. The Connie rolled violently. Tubes flared as the pilot fought to correct the roll. He slowed the spinning as Rip and Santos passed, just long enough for a Connie gunner to get in a final shot.

The shell struck directly under Rip. He felt himself pushed violently upward, and at the same moment he reacted, by hunch and not by reason. He rammed the controls full ahead and the dying rocket cut space, curving slowly as flaming fuel spurted from the ruptured tanks.

Rip yelled, "Santos! You all right?"

"I think so. Lieutenant, we're on fire!"

"I know it. Get ready to abandon ship."

When the main mass of fuel caught, the rocket would become an inferno. Rip smashed at the escape hatch above his head, grabbed propulsion tubes from the rack and called, "Now!"

He pulled the release on his harness, stood up on the seat, and thrust with all his leg power. He catapulted out of the burning snapper-boat into space.

Santos followed a second later and the crippled rocket twisted wildly under the two Planeteers.

"Don't use the propulsion tubes," Rip called. "Slow down with your air bottles." He thrust the tubes into his belt, found his air bottles, and pointed two of them in the direction they had been traveling. He wanted to come to a stop, to let the wild snapper-boat get away from them.

The compressed air bottles did the trick. He and Santos slowed down as the little jets overcame the inertia that was taking them along with the burning boat. The boat was spiraling now, and burning freely. It moved away from them, its stern jets firing weakly as fuel burned in the tank.

Rip took a look toward the enemy cruiser. The assault boat was no longer showing an exhaust. Instead, it was being dragged rapidly away from the Connie cruiser by the pull of the sun. At least they had hit it in time to prevent launching of the atomic guided missiles. Or, he thought, perhaps the enemy had never intended using them. The principal effect, besides killing the Planeteers, would have been to drive the asteroid into the sun at an even faster rate.

The enemy assault boat was no longer a menace. Its occupants would be lucky if they succeeded in saving their own lives.

Rip wondered what the Connie cruiser commander would try now. Only one thing remained, and

Rip and Santos Fell Through Space

that was to set the cruiser down on the asteroid. If the Connie tried, he would arrive at just about the time set for releasing the nuclear charge. And that would be the end of the cruiser—and probably of the Planeteers as well.

Santos asked coolly, "Lieutenant, wouldn't you say we're in sort of a bad spot?"

Rip had been so busy sizing up the situation that he hadn't thought about his own predicament. Now he looked down and suddenly realized that he was floating free in space, a considerable distance above the asteroid, and with only small propulsion tubes for power.

He gasped, "Great space! We're in a mess, Santos."

The Filipino corporal asked, still in a calm voice, "How long before we're dragged into the sun, sir?"

Rip stared. Santos had used the same tone he might have used in asking for a piece of Venusian *chru*. An officer couldn't be less calm, so Rip replied in a voice he hoped was casual, "I wouldn't worry, Santos. We won't know it. The heat will get through our suits long before then."

In fact, the heat should be overloading their ventilating systems right now. In a few minutes the cooling elements would break down and that would be the end. He listened for the accelerated whine as the ventilating system struggled under the increased heat load, and heard nothing.

Funny. Had it overloaded and given out already?

No, that was impossible. He would be feeling the heat on his body if that were the case.

He looked for an explanation and realized for the first time that they weren't in the sunlight at all. They were in darkness. His searching glance told him they were in the cone of shadow stretching out from behind the asteroid. The thorium rock was between them and the sun!

His lips moved soundlessly. Major Joe Barris had been right! *In a jam, trust your hunch.* He had acted instinctively, not even thinking what he was doing as he used the last full power of the stern tubes to throw them into the shadow cone.

And he knew in the same moment that it could save their lives. The sun's pull would only accelerate their fall toward the asteroid. He said exultantly, "We're staying out of high vack, Santos. Light off a propulsion tube. Let's get back to the asteroid."

He pulled a tube from his belt, held it above his head, and thumbed the striker mechanism. The tube flared, pushing downward on his hand. He held steady and plummeted feet first toward the rock.

Santos was only a few seconds behind him. Rip saw the corporal's tube flare and knew that everything was all right, at least for the moment, even though the asteroid was still a long way down.

He looked upward at the Connie cruiser and saw that it was moving. Its exhaust increased in length and deepened slightly in color as Rip watched, his

forehead creased in a frown. What was the Connie
up to?

· Then he saw side jets flare out from the projecting
control tubes and knew the ship was maneuvering.
Rip realized suddenly that the cruiser was going to
pick up the crippled assault boat.

He hadn't expected such a humane move after his
first meeting with the Connie cruiser when the commander had been willing to sacrifice his own men.
This time, however, there was a difference, he saw.
The commander would lose nothing by picking up
the assault boat, and he would save a few men. Rip
supposed that manpower meant something, even to
Consops.

His propulsion tube reached brennschluss, and
for a few moments he watched, checking his speed
and direction. Then, before he lit off another tube,
he checked his chronometer. The illuminated dial
registered 2301. They had just four minutes to get
to the asteroid!

He spoke swiftly. "Waste no time in lighting off,
Santos. That nuclear charge goes in four minutes!"

The Filipino corporal said merely, "Yessir."

Rip pulled a tube from his belt, held it overhead,
and triggered it. His flight through space speeded
up but he wasn't at all sure they would make it. He
turned up his helmet communicator to full power
and called, "Koa, can you hear me?"

The sergeant-major's reply was faint in his helmet.

"I hear you weakly. Do you hear me?"

"Same way," Rip replied. "Get this, Koa. Don't fail to explode that charge at twenty-three-oh-five. Can you see us?"

The reply was very slightly stronger. "I will explode the charge as ordered, Lieutenant. We can see a pair of rocket exhausts, but no boats. Is that you?"

"Yes. We're coming in on propulsion tubes."

Koa waited for a long moment, then: "Sir, what if you're not with us by twenty-three-oh-five?"

"You know the answer," Rip retorted crisply.

Of course Koa knew. The nuclear blast would send Rip and Santos spinning into outer space, perhaps crippled, burned, or completely irradiated. But the lives of two men couldn't delay the blast that would save the lives of eight others, not counting prisoners.

Rip estimated his speed and course and the distance to the asteroid. He was increasingly sure that they wouldn't make it, and the knowledge was like the cold of space in his stomach. It would be close, but not close enough. A minute would make all the difference.

For a few heartbeats he almost called Koa and told him to wait that extra minute, to explode the nuclear charge at 2306, at the very last second. But even Planeteer chronometers could be off by a few seconds and he couldn't risk it. His men had to be given some leeway.

The decision made, he put his mind to the problem. There must be some way out. There must be!

He surveyed the asteroid. The nuclear charge was on his left side, pretty close to the sun line. At least he and Santos could angle to the right, to get as far away from the blast as possible.

The edge of the asteroid's shadow was barely visible. That it was visible at all was due to the minute particles of matter and gas that surrounded the sun, even millions of miles out into space. He reduced helmet power and told Santos, "Angle to the right. Get as close to the edge of shadow as you can without being cooked."

As an afterthought, he asked, "How many tubes do you have?"

"One after this, sir. I had three."

Rip also had one left. That was correct, because snapper-boats carried three in each man's position.

"Save the one you have left," he ordered.

He didn't know yet what use they would be, but it was always a good idea to have some kind of reserve.

The Connie cruiser was sliding up to the crippled assault boat. Rip took a quick look, then shifted his hands, and angled toward the edge of shadow. When he was within a few feet he reversed the direction of the tube to keep from shooting out into sunlight. A second or two later the tube burned out.

Santos was several yards away and slightly above

him. Rip saw that the Planeteer was all right and turned his attention to the cruiser once more. It was close enough to the assault boat to haul it in with grappling hooks. The hooks emerged and engaged the torn metal of the boat, then drew it into the waiting port. The massive air door slid closed.

The question was, would the Connie try to set his ship down on the asteroid? Rip grinned without mirth. Now would be a fine time. His chronometer showed a minute and half to blast time.

He took another look at his own situation. He and Santos were getting close to the asteroid, but there was still over a half mile earth distance to go. They would cover perhaps three-fourths of that distance before Koa fired the charge.

He had a daring idea. How long could he and Santos last in direct sunlight? The effect of the sun in the open was powerful enough to make lead run like water. Their suits could absorb some heat and the ventilating system could take care of quite a lot. They might last as much as three minutes, with luck.

They had to take a risk with the full knowledge that the odds were against them. But if they didn't take the risk, the blast would push them outward from the asteroid—into full sunlight. The end result would be the same.

"We're not going to make it, Santos," he began.

"I know it, sir," Santos replied.

Rip thought, anyone with that much coolness and

sheer nerve rated some kind of special treatment. And the Filipino corporal had shown his ability time and time again. He said, "I should have known you knew, *Sergeant* Santos. We still have a slight chance. When I give the word, use an air bottle to push you into the sunlight. When I give the word again, light off your remaining tube."

"Yessir," Santos replied. "Thank you for the promotion. I hope I live to collect the extra rating."

"Same here," Rip agreed fervently. His eyes were on his chronometer, and with his free hand he took another air bottle. When the chronometer registered exactly one minute before blast time, he called, "Now!" He triggered the bottle and moved from shadow into glaring sunlight. A slight motion of the bottle turned him so his back was to the sun, then he used the remaining compressed air to push him downward along the edge of shadow. The sun's gravity tugged at him.

He pulled the last tube from his belt and held it ready while he watched his chronometer creep around. With five seconds to go, he called to Santos and fired it. Acceleration pushed at him.

In the same moment, the nuclear charge exploded.

CHAPTER SIXTEEN

RIDE THE GRAY PLANET!

A mighty hand reached out and shoved Rip, sweeping him through space like a dust mote. He clutched his propulsion tube with both hands and fought to hold it steady.

He swiveled his head quickly, searching for Santos, and saw the Filipino a dozen rods away, still holding fast to his tube.

From the far horizon of the asteroid the incandescent fire of the nuclear blast stretched into space, turning from silver to orange to red as it cooled.

Rip knew they had escaped the heat and blast of the explosion, but there was a question of how much of the prompt radiation they had absorbed. During the first few seconds, a nuclear blast vomited gamma radiation and neutrons in all directions. He and Santos certainly had gotten plenty. But how much? Putting their dosimeters into a measuring meter aboard a cruiser would tell them. His low-level colorimeter had long since reached maximum red, and his high-level dosimeter could be read only on a measuring device.

Meanwhile, he had other worries. Radiation had no immediate effect. At worst, it would be a few hours before he felt any symptoms.

As he sized up his position and that of the aster-oid, he let out a yell of triumph. His gamble would succeed! He had estimated that going into the direct gravity pull of the sun at the proper moment, and lighting off their last tubes, would put them into a landing position. The asteroid was swerving rapidly, moving into a new orbit that would intersect the course he and Santos were on. He had planned on the asteroid's change of orbit. In a minute at most they would be back on the rock.

His propulsion tube flared out and he released it. It would travel along with him, but his hands would be free. He watched closely as the asteroid drew nearer and estimated they would land with plenty of room to spare.

Then he saw something else. The blast had started the asteroid turning!

He reacted instantly. Turning up his communi-cator he yelled, "Koa! The rock is spinning! Cut the prisoners loose, grab the equipment, and run for it! You'll have to keep running to stay in the shadow. If sunlight hits those fuel tanks or the tubes of rocket fuel, they'll explode!"

Koa replied tersely, "Got it. We're moving."

The Planeteers and their prisoners would have to move fast, running to stay out of direct sunlight. A moment or two in the sun wouldn't hurt the men, but the chemical fuels in the cutting tanks and rocket tubes would explode in a matter of seconds.

At least the Connie cruiser couldn't harm them now, Rip thought grimly. He looked for the cruiser and failed to find it for several seconds. It had moved. He finally saw its exhausts some distance away.

He forgot his own predicament in a grin. The Connie cruiser had moved, but not because its commander had wanted to. It had been right in the path of the nuclear blast, although some distance from it. The Connie had been literally shoved away.

Then Rip forgot the cruiser. His suit ventilator was whining under the terrific heat and his whole body was bathed in perspiration. The sun was getting them. It was only a short time until the ventilator overloaded and burned out. They had to reach the asteroid before then. The trouble was, there was nothing further he could do about it. He had only air bottles left, and their blast was so weak that the effect wouldn't speed him up much. Nevertheless, he called to Santos and directed him to use his bottles. Then he did the same.

Santos spoke up. "Sir, we're going to make it."

In the same instant, Rip saw that they would land on the dark side. The asteroid was turning over and over, and for a second he had the impression he was looking at a turning globe of the earth, the kind used in elementary school back home. But this gray planet was scarcely bigger than the giant globe at the entrance of the Space Council building on Terra.

The gray metal world suddenly leaped into sharp focus and seemed to rush toward him. It was an optical illusion. The ability of the eyes to perceive depth sharply—the faculty known as depth perception—didn't appear to operate normally until the eyes were within a certain distance of an object.

He knew he was going to hit hard. The way to keep from being hurt was to turn the vertical energy of his arrival into motion in another direction. As he swept down to the metal surface he started running, his legs pumping wildly in space. He hit with a bone-jarring thud, lost his footing and fell sideways, both hands cradling his helmet. He got to his feet instantly and looked for Santos. A good thing his equipment was shock-mounted, he thought. Otherwise the communicator would be knocked for a line of galaxies.

"You all right, sir?" Santos called anxiously.

"Yes. Are you?"

"I'm fine. I think the others are over there." He pointed.

"We'll find them," Rip said. His hip hurt like fury from smashing against the unyielding metal, and the worst part was that he couldn't rub it. The blow had been strong enough to hurt through the heavy fabric and air pressure, but his hand wasn't strong enough to compress the suit. Just the same, he tried.

And while he was trying, he found himself in direct sunlight!

He had forgotten to run. Standing still on the
asteroid meant turning with it, from darkness into
sunlight and back again. He yelled at Santos and
legged it out of there, moving in long, gliding steps.
He regained the shadow and kept going.

The first order of business was to stop the rock
from turning. Otherwise they couldn't live on it.

Rip knew that they had only one means of stopping the spin. That was to use the tubes of rocket
fuel left over from correcting the course. They had
three tubes left, but he didn't know if that was
enough to do the job.

Moving rapidly, he and Santos caught up to Koa
and the Planeteers.

The Connie prisoners were pretty well bunched
up, gliding along like a herd of fantastic sheep. Their
shepherds were Pederson, Nunez, and Dowst. The
three Planeteers had a pistol in each hand. The
spares were probably those taken from prisoners.

The Planeteers were loaded down with equipment. A few Connie prisoners carried equipment,
too.

Trudeau had the rocket launcher and the remaining rockets. Kemp had his torch and two tanks of
oxygen. Bradshaw had tied his safety line to the
squat containers of chemical fuel for the torch and
was towing them behind like strange balloons. The
only trouble with that system, Rip thought, was that
Bradshaw could stop, but the containers would have

a tendency to keep going. Unless the English Planeteer were skillful, his burdens would drag him
right off his feet.

Dominico had a tube of rocket fuel under each
arm. The Italian was small and the tubes were
bulky. Each was about ten feet long and two feet in
diameter. With any gravity or air resistance at all,
the Italian couldn't have carried even one.

Rip smiled as Dominico glided along. He looked
as though the tubes were floating him over the asteroid, instead of the other way around.

Santos took the radiation detection instruments
and the case with the astrogation equipment from
Koa. Rip greeted his men briefly, then took his
computing board and began figuring. He knew the
men were glad he and Santos had made it. But they
kept their greetings short. A spinning asteroid was
no place for long and sentimental speeches.

He remembered the dimensions of the asteroid
and its mass. He computed its inertia, then figured
out what it would take to overcome the inertia of
the spin.

The mathematics would have been simple under
normal conditions, but doing them on the run, trying to watch his step at the same time, made things
a little complicated. He had to hold the board under
his arm, run alongside Santos while the new sergeant
held the case open, select the book he wanted, open
it and try to read the tables by his belt light and

then transfer the data to the board.

His ventilator had quieted down once he got into the darkness, but now it started whining slightly again because he was sweating profusely. Finally he figured out the thrust needed to stop the spin. Now all he had to do was compute how much fuel it would take.

He had figures on the amount of thrust given by the kind of rocket fuel in the tubes. He also knew how much fuel each tube contained. But the figures were not in his head. They were on reference sheets.

He collected the data on the fly, slowing down now and then to read something, until a yell from Santos or Koa warned that the sun line was creeping close. When he had all data noted on the board, he started his mathematics. He was right in the middle of a laborious equation when he stumbled over a thorium crystal. He went headlong, shooting like a rocket three feet above the ground. His board flew away at a tangent. His stylus sped out of his glove like a miniature projectile, and the slide rule clanged against his bubble.

It happened so fast neither Koa nor Santos had time to grab him. The action had given him extra speed and he saw with horror that he was going to crash into Trudeau. He yelled, "Frenchy! Watch out!" Then put both hands before him to protect his helmet. His hands caught the French Planeteer between the shoulders with a bone-jarring thud.

CHAPTER SEVENTEEN

THE ARCHER AND THE EAGLE

Trudeau held tight to the launcher, but the rocket racks opened and spilled attack rockets into space. They flew in a dozen different directions. Trudeau gave vent to his feelings in colorful French.

Koa and Santos laughed so hard they had trouble collecting the scattered equipment. Rip, slowed by his crash with Trudeau, got his feet under him again.

The asteroid had turned into the sun before they collected everything but Rip's stylus and five attack rockets. The space-pencil was the only thing that could write on the computing board. It had to be found.

"Next time around," Rip called to the others, and led the way full speed ahead until they regained the safety of shadow.

Rip suspected the stylus was somewhere above the rock and probably wouldn't return to the surface for some minutes. While he was wondering what to do, there was a chorus of yells. A rocket sped between the Planeteers and shot off into space.

"Our own rockets are after us," Trudeau gasped. There hadn't been time to collect them all after Rip's unwilling attack on the Frenchman scattered them. Now the sun was setting them off. Another flashed past, fortunately over their heads. The sun's heat was causing them to fire unevenly. Rip hoped they would all go off soon and get it over with.

"Three more to go," Koa called. "Watch out!"

Only two went, and they were far enough away to offer no danger.

Santos had been fishing around in the instrument case. He triumphantly produced another stylus. "It was under the sextant," he explained. "I thought there was another one around somewhere."

"If we get through this I'll propose you for ten more stripes," Rip vowed. "We'll make you the highest ranking sergeant that ever made a private's life miserable."

Working slowly but more safely, Rip figured that slightly more than two and a half tubes would do the trick.

Now to fire them. That meant finding a thorium crystal properly placed and big enough. There were plenty of crystals, so that was no problem. The next step was for Kemp to cut holes with his torch, so that the thrust of the rocket fuel would be counter to the direction in which the asteroid was spinning.

Rip explained to all hands what had to be done. The burden would fall on Kemp, who would need a helper. Rip took that job himself. He took one oxygen tank from Kemp. Koa took the other, leaving the torchman with only his torch.

Then Rip took a container of chemical fuel from Bradshaw. Working while running, he lashed the two containers together with his safety line. Then he improvised a rope sling so they could hang on his back. He wanted his hands free.

Kemp, meanwhile, assembled his torch and put the proper cutting nozzle in place. When he was ready, he moved to Rip's side and connected the hoses of the torch to the tanks the lieutenant carried. Kemp had the torch mechanism strapped to his own back. It was essentially a high pressure pump that drew oxygen and fuel from the tanks and forced them through the nozzle under terrific pressure.

When he had finished, he pressed the trigger that started the cutting torch going. The fuel ignited about a half inch in front of the nozzle. The nozzle had two holes in it, one for oxygen and the other for fuel. The holes were placed and angled to keep the flame always a half inch away, otherwise the nozzle itself would melt.

"How do we work this?" Kemp asked.

"We'll get ahead of the others," Rip explained. "Keep up speed until we're running at the forward sun line. Then, when the crystal we want comes around into the shadow, we can stop running and work until it spins into the sunshine again."

"Got it," Kemp agreed.

Rip estimated the axis on which the asteroid was spinning and selected a crystal in the right position.

He had to be careful, otherwise their counter-blast might do nothing more than start the gray planet wobbling.

He and Kemp ran ahead of the others. The Planeteers and their prisoners were running at a speed that kept them right in the middle of the dark area.

It was like running on a treadmill. The Planeteers were making good speed, but were actually staying in the same place relative to the sun's position, keeping the turning asteroid between them and the sun.

Rip and Kemp ran forward until they were right at the sun line. Then they slowed down, holding position and waiting for the crystal they had chosen to reach them. As it came across the sun line into darkness they stopped running and rode the crystal through the shadow until it reached the sun again. Then the two Planeteers ran back across the dark zone to meet the crystal as it came around again. There was only a few minutes' working time each revolution.

Kemp worked fast, and the first hole deepened. Rip helped as best he could by pushing away the chunks of thorium that Kemp cut free, but it was essentially a one-man job.

As Kemp neared the bottom of the first hole, Rip reviewed his plan and realized he had overlooked something. These weren't nuclear bombs; they were simple tubes of chemical fuel. The tubes wouldn't destroy the hole Kemp was cutting.

He reached a quick decision and called Koa to join them. Koa appeared as Kemp pulled his torch from the hole and started running again to avoid the sun. Rip and Koa ran right along with him, crossing the dark zone to meet the crystal as it came around again.

"There's no reason to drill three holes," Rip explained as they ran. "We'll use one hole for all three charges. They don't have to be fired all at once."

"How do we fire them?" Koa asked.

"Electrically. Who has the exploders and the hand dynamo?"

"Dowst has the exploders. One of the Connies is carrying the dynamo."

Speaking of the Connies . . . Rip hadn't seen the Consops cruiser recently. He looked up, searching for its exhaust, and finally found it, a faint line some distance away.

The Connie commander was stalemated for the time being. He couldn't land his cruiser on a spinning asteroid, and he had no more boats. Rip thought he probably was just waiting around for any opportunity that might present itself.

The Federation cruisers should be arriving. He studied his chronometer. No, the nearest one, the *Sagittarius* from Mercury, wasn't due for another ten minutes or so. He turned up his helmet communicator and ordered all hands to watch for the exhaust of a nuclear drive cruiser, then turned it down again and gave Koa instructions.

"Have Trudeau turn his load over to a Connie and collect the exploders and the dynamo. We'll need wire, too. Who has that?"

"Another Connie."

"Get a reel. Cut off a few hundred feet and connect the dynamo to one end and an exploder to the other."

The crystal came around again and Kemp got to work. Rip stood by, again reviewing all steps. They couldn't afford to make a mistake. He had no margin of error.

Kemp finished the hole a few seconds before the crystal turned into the sunlight again. Rip told him to keep the torch going. There might be some last minute cutting to do. Then the lieutenant hurried off at an angle to where Dominico was plodding along with the fuel tubes.

Koa had turned the tube he carried over to a Connie. Rip got it, and told Dominico to follow him. Then he angled back across the asteroid to where Kemp was holding position.

The asteroid turned twice before Koa arrived. He had a coil of wire slung over his arm and he carried the dynamo in one hand and an exploder in the other, the two connected by the wire.

Rip took the exploder. "Uncoil the wire," he directed. "Go to its full length at right angles to the hole. We have to time this exactly right. When the crystal comes around again, I'll shove the tube into the hole, then scurry for cover. When I'm clear I'll yell and you pump the dynamo. Dominico and Kemp stay with Koa. Make sure no one is in the way of the blast."

Koa unreeled the wire, moving away from Rip. The lieutenant pushed the exploder into one end of the fuel tube and crimped it tightly with his gloved hand.

Koa and the others were as far away as they could get now, the wire stretching between them and Rip. Kemp had made sure no one was running near the line of blast.

Rip watched for the crystal. It would be coming around any second now. He held the tube with the exploder projecting behind him, ready for the hole to appear.

Koa's voice echoed in his helmet. "All set, Lieutenant."

"So am I," Rip answered. "Stand by."

The crystal appeared across the sun line and moved toward him. He met it, slowed his speed, put the end of the tube into the hole and shoved. Kemp had allowed enough clearance. The tube slid into place. Rip turned and angled off as fast as he could glide. When he was far enough away from the blast line he called, "Fire!"

Koa squeezed the dynamo handle. The machine

"Fire!" Called Rip

whined and current shot through the wire. A column of orange fire spurted from the crystal.

Rip watched the stars instead of the exhaust. He kept running as it burned soundlessly. In air, the noise would have deafened him. In airless space, there was nothing to carry the sound.

The apparent motion of the stars was definitely slowing. The spinning wouldn't cease entirely, but it would slow down enough to give them more time to work.

The tube reached brennschluss and Rip called orders. "Same process. Get ready to repeat. Dominico, bring one of your tubes."

While Koa was connecting another exploder to the wire, Rip took a tube from Dominico. "Take your space knife and saw through the tube you have left. We'll need about three-fifths of it. Keep both pieces."

Dominico pulled his knife, pressed the release, and the gas capsule shot the blade out. He got to work.

Koa called that he was ready. Rip took the wired exploder from him and thrust it into the tube Dominico had given him.

As the crystal came around again, the process was repeated. The hole was undamaged.

There was more time to get clear because of the asteroid's slower speed. The second tube slowed the rock even more, so that they had to wait long minutes while the crystal came around again.

Rip did some estimating. He wanted to be sure
the next charge would do nothing more than slow
the asteroid to a stop. If the charge were too heavy,
it would reverse the spin. He didn't want to make
a career of running on the asteroid. He was tired
and he knew his men were getting weary, too. He
could see it in their strides—they were less sure of
foot.

He decided it would be best to use a little less
fuel rather than a little more. If the asteroid failed
to stop its spin completely, they could always set off
a small charge or two.

"Hold it," he ordered. "We'll use the small end
of Dominico's tube and save the big one."

The fuel was a solid mass, so cutting the tube in
two sections caused no difficulty. Rip pushed the
exploder into the small section, seated it in the hole,
and hurried to cover. As he watched the fuel burn,
he wondered why the last nuclear charge had started
the spin. He had made a mistake somewhere. The
earlier blasts had been set so they wouldn't cause a
spin. He made a mental note to look at the place
where the charge had exploded when things were
more quiet.

The rocket fuel slowed the asteroid down to a
point where it was barely turning, and Rip was glad
he had been cautious. The heavier charge would
have reversed it a little. He directed the placing of

a very small charge and was moving away from it so Koa could set it off when Santos suddenly yelled, "Sir! The Connie is coming!"

Rip called, "Fire the charge, Koa," then looked up. The Consops cruiser was moving slowly toward them. The canny Connie had been waiting for something to happen on the asteroid, Rip guessed. When the spinning slowed and then stopped, the Connie probably had decided that now was the time for a final try.

"Where is the communicator?" Rip asked Koa.

"One of the Connies has it."

"Get it. I'll notify Terra base of what happened."

Koa found the Connie with the communicator, tested it to be sure the prisoner hadn't sabotaged it, and brought it to Rip.

"This is Foster to Terra base. **Over.**"

"Come in, Foster."

Rip explained briefly what had happened and asked, "How is our orbit? I haven't had time to take sightings."

"You're free of the sun," Terra base answered. "Your orbit will have to be corrected sometime within the next few hours. The last blast pushed you off course."

"That's a small matter," Rip stated. "Unless we can think of something fast, this will be a Connie asteroid by then. The Consops cruiser is moving in on us. He's careful, because he isn't sure of the situation. But even at his present speed he'll be here in ten minutes."

"Stand by." Terra base was silent for a few moments, then the voice replied. "I think we have an answer for you, Foster. Terra base off. Go ahead, MacFife."

A Scottish burr thick enough to saw boards came out of the communicator. "Foster, this is MacFife, commander of the *Aquila*. Y'can't see me on account of I'm on yer sunny side. But, lad, I'm closer to ye than the Connie. We did it this way to keep the asteroid between us and him. Also, lad, if ye'll take a look up at Gemini, ye'll see somethin' ye'll like. Look at Alhena, in the Twins' feet. Then, lad, if ye'll be patient the while, ye'll have a grandstand seat for a real big show."

Rip tilted his bubble back and stared upward at the constellation of the twins. He said softly, "By Gemini!" For there, a half degree south of the star Alhena, was the clean line of a nuclear cruiser's exhaust. The *Sagittarius,* out of Mercury, had arrived.

He cut the communicator off for a moment and spoke exultantly to his men. "Stand easy, you hairy Planeteers. Forget the Connie. He doesn't know it, but he's caught. He's caught between the Archer and the Eagle!"

CHAPTER EIGHTEEN

COURTESY—WITH CLAWS

Sagittarius, constellation of the Archer, and *Aquila,* constellation of the Eagle, had given the two Federation patrol cruisers their names. The Eagle was commanded by a tough Scotsman, and the Archer by a Frenchman.

Commander MacFife spoke through the communicator. "Switch bands to universal, lad. Me'n Galliene are goin' to talk this Connie into a braw mess. MacFife off."

Rip guessed that the two cruiser commanders had been in communication while enroute to the asteroid and had cooked up some kind of plan. He turned the band switch to the universal frequency with which all long-range communicators were equipped. Each of the earth groups had its own frequency, and so did the Martians and Jovians. But all could meet and talk on the universal band.

Special scrambling devices prevented eavesdropping on regular frequencies, so there was no danger that the Connie had overheard the plan. Rip wondered what it was. He knew the cruisers had to be careful not to cross the thin line that might lead to war.

The *Sagittarius* loomed closer, decelerating with a tremendous exhaust. The Connie couldn't have failed to see it, Rip knew. He was right. The Consops cruiser suddenly blasted more heavily, rushing in the direction away from the Federation ship. The direction was toward the asteroid.

And at the same moment, the *Aquila* flashed above the horizon, also decelerating. The Connie was caught squarely.

A suave voice spoke on the universal band. "This is Federation *SCN Sagittarius,* calling the Consolidation cruiser near the asteroid. Please reply."

Rip waited anxiously. The Connie would hear, because every control room monitored the universal band.

A heavy, reluctant voice replied after a pause of over a minute.

"This is Consolidation cruiser Sixteen. You are breaking the law, *Sagittarius.* Your missile ports are open and they are pointing at me. Close them at once or I will report this."

The suave voice with its hint of French accent replied, "Ah, my friend! Do not be alarmed. We have had a slight accident to our control circuit and the ports are jammed open. We are trying to repair the situation. But I assure you, we have only the friendliest of intentions."

Rip grinned. This was about the same as a man holding a cocked pistol at another man's head and assuring him it was nothing but a nervous arm that kept the gun so steady.

The Connie demanded, "What do you want?"

The two friendly cruisers were within a few miles of the Connie now and their blasts were just strong enough to keep them edging closer, while counteracting the sun's pull.

The French spaceman spoke reassuringly. "My friend, we want only the courtesy of space to which the law entitles us. We have had an unfortunate accident to our astrogation instruments, and we wish to come aboard to compare them with yours."

Rip laughed outright. Every cruiser carried at least four full sets of instruments. There was as much chance of all of them being knocked off scale at once as there was of his biting a cruiser in half with bare teeth.

MacFife's voice came on the air. "Foster. Switch to Federation frequency."

Rip did so. "This is Foster, Commander."

"Lad, it's a pity for ye to miss the show. I'm sending a boat for ye."

"The sun will get it!" Rip exclaimed.

"Never fear, lad. It won't get this one. Now switch back to universal and listen in."

Rip did so in time to catch the Connie commander's voice. ". . . and I refuse to believe such a story! Great Cosmos, do you think I am a fool?"

"Of course not," the Frenchman replied. "You

are not such a fool as to refuse a simple request to check our instruments."

The *Sagittarius* commander was right. Rip understood the strategy. Equipment sometimes did go out of operation in space, and Connies had no hesitation in asking Federation cruisers for help, or the other way around. Such help was always given, because no commander could be sure when he might need help himself.

"I agree," the Connie commander said with obvious reluctance. "You may send a boat."

MacFife's Scotch burr broke in. "Federation *SCN Aquila* to Consolidation Sixteen. Mister, my instruments are off scale, too. I'll just send them along to ye and ye can check them while ye're doing the *Sagittarius!*"

"I object!" the Connie bellowed.

"Come now," MacFife burred soothingly. "Checking a few instruments won't hurt ye."

A small rocket exhaust appeared, leaving the *Aquila*. The exhaust grew rapidly, more rapidly than that of any snapper-boat. Rip watched it, while keeping his ears tuned to the space conversation.

Koa tugged his arm. "See that, sir?"

Rip nodded.

"Surely sending boats is too much of a nuisance," the French commander said winningly. "We will come alongside."

"It's a trick," the Connie growled. "You want me

to open my valves, then your men will board us and try to take over my ship!"

"My friend, you have a suspicious mind," Galliene replied smoothly. "If you wish, arm your men. Ours will have no weapons. Train launchers on the valves so our men will be annihilated before they can board, if you see a single weapon."

This was going a little far, Rip thought, but it was not his affair and he didn't know exactly what MacFife and Galliene had in mind.

The *Aquila's* boat arrived with astonishing speed. Rip saw it flash in the sunlight and knew he had never seen one like it before. It was a perfect globe, about 20 feet in diameter. Blast holes covered the globe at intervals of six feet.

The boat settled to the asteroid and a new voice called over the helmet circuit, "Where's Foster? Show an exhaust! We're in a rush."

Rip ordered, "Take over, Koa. I'll be back."

"Yessir."

He hurried to the boat and stood there, bewildered. He didn't know how to get in.

"Up here," the voice called. He looked up and saw a hatch. He jumped and a space-clad figure pulled him inside. The door shut and the boat blasted off. Acceleration shoved him backward, but the spaceman snapped a line to his belt, then motioned him to a seat. Rip pulled himself up the line and got into the seat, snapping the harness in place.

"I'm Hawkins, senior space officer," the spaceman said. "Welcome, Foster. We've been losing weight wondering if we'd get here in time."

"I was never so glad to see spacemen in my life," Rip said truthfully. "What kind of craft is this, sir?"

"Experimental," the space officer answered. "It has a number, but we call it the ball-bat because it's shaped like a ball and goes like a bat. We were about to take off for some test runs around the space platform when we got a hurry call to come here. The *Aquila* has two of these. If they prove out, they'll replace the snapper-boats. More power, greater maneuverability, heavier weapons, and they carry more men."

There was only the officer and a pilot, but Rip saw positions for several others.

He looked out through the port and saw the two Federation cruisers closing in on the Connie. Apparently the Connie commander had agreed to let the cruisers come alongside.

The ball-bat blasted to the *Aquila,* paused at an open port, then slid inside. The valve was shut before Rip could unbuckle his harness. Air flooded into the chamber and the lights flicked on. The space officer gave Rip a hand out of the harness, and the young Planeteer went through the hatch to the deck.

The inner valve opened and a lean, sandy-haired officer in space blue with the insignia of a commander stepped through. Grinning, he hurried to Rip's side and twisted his bubble, lifting it off.

"Hurry, lad," he greeted Rip. "I'm MacFife. Get out of that suit quick, because ye don't want to miss what's aboot to happen." With his own hands he unlocked the complicated belt with its gadgets and equipment, disconnected the communicator and ventilator, and then unfastened the lock clips that held top and bottom of the suit together.

Rip slipped the upper part over his head and stepped out of the bottom. "Thanks, Commander. I'm one grateful Planeteer, believe me!"

"Come on. We'll hurry right across ship to the opposite valve. Lad, I've a son in the Planeteers and he's just about your own age. He's on Ganymede. He and the others will be proud of what ye've done."

MacFife was pulling himself along rapidly by the convenient handholds. Rip followed, his breathing a little rapid in the heavier air of the ship. He followed the Scottish commander through the maze of passages that crossed the ship and stopped at a valve where spacemen were waiting. With them was an officer who carried a big case.

"The instruments," MacFife said, pointing. "We've tinkered with them a bit just to make it look real."

"But why do you want to board the Connie?" Rip asked curiously.

MacFife's eye closed in a wink. "Ye'll see."

There was a slight bump as the cruiser touched the Connie. The waiting group recovered balance and faced the valve. Rip knew that spacemen in the inner lock were making fast to the Connie cruiser, setting up the airtight seal.

It wasn't long before a bell sounded and a spaceman opened the inner valve. Two men in space suits were waiting, and beyond them the outer valve was joined by a tube to the outer valve of the Connie ship. Rip stared at the Connie spacemen in their red tunics and gray trousers. One, a scowling officer with two pistols in his belt, stepped forward.

Rip noted that the other Connies were heavy with weapons, too. None of his group had any.

"I'm the commander," the scowling Connie said. "Bring your instruments in quickly. We will check them, then you get out."

"Ye're no verra friendly," MacFife said, his burr even more pronounced. He led Rip and the officer with the instruments into the Connie ship.

A handsome Federation spaceman with a mustache, the first Rip had ever seen, stepped into the room from a passageway on the opposite side. The spaceman bowed with exquisite grace. "I have the honor of making myself known," he proclaimed. "Commander Rémy Galliene of the *Sagittarius.*"

The Connie commander grunted. He was afraid, Rip realized. The Connie suspected a trick, and he had no idea of what it might be.

Rip looked him over with interest. This was the man who had been willing to burn his own spacemen back at the asteroid belt.

Galliene saw Rip's black uniform and hurried to shake his hand. "So this is the young lieutenant who is responsible! Lieutenant, today the spacemen honor the Planeteers because of you. Most days we fight each other, but today we fight together, eh? I am glad to meet you!"

"And I'm glad to meet you, sir," Rip returned. He liked the twinkle in the Frenchman's eye. He would have given a lot to know what scheme Galliene and MacFife had cooked up.

The Connie had overheard Galliene's greeting. He glared at Rip. The Frenchman saw the look and smiled happily. "Ah, you do not know each other? Commander, I have the honor to make known Lieutenant Foster of the Federation Special Order Squadrons. He is in command on the asteroid."

The Connie blurted, "So! I send boats to help you and you fire on them!"

So that was to be the Consops story! Rip thought quickly, then held up his hand in a shocked gesture that would have done credit to the Frenchman. "Oh, no, Commander! You misunderstand. We had no way of communicating by radio, so I did the only thing we could do. I fired rockets as a warning. We didn't want your boats to get caught in a nuclear explosion." He shrugged. "It was very unlucky for us that the sun threw my gunner's aim off and he hit your boats, quite by accident."

MacFife coughed to cover up a chuckle. Galliene hid a smile by stroking his mustache.

The Connie commander growled, "And I suppose it was accident that you took my men prisoner?"

"Prisoner?" Rip looked bewildered. "We took no prisoners. When your boats arrived, the men asked if they might not join us. They claimed refuge, which we had to give them under interplanetary law."

"I will take them back," the Connie stated.

"You will not," Galliene replied with equal positiveness. "The law is very clear, my friend. Your men may return willingly, but you cannot force them. When we reach Terra we will give them a choice. Those who wish to return to the Consolidation will be given transportation to the nearest border."

The Connie commander motioned to a heavily armed officer. "Take their instruments. Check them quickly." He put his lips together in a straight line and stared at the Federation men. They stared back with equal coldness. Around them, Connie spacemen with wooden, expressionless faces waited without moving.

The minutes ticked by. Rip wondered again what kind of plan MacFife and Galliene had. When would the excitement start?

Additional minutes passed and the officer returned with the cases. Wordlessly he handed them to Galliene and MacFife. The Connie commander snapped, "There. Now get out of my ship."

Galliene bowed. "You have been a most courteous and gracious host," he said. "Your conversation has been stimulating, inspiring, and informative. Our profound thanks."

He shook hands with Rip and MacFife, bowed to the Connie commander again, and went out the way he had come. There wasn't anything to say after the Frenchman's sarcastic farewell speech. MacFife, Rip, and the officer with the instruments went back through the valves into their own ship.

Once inside, MacFife called, "Come with me. Hurry." He led the way through passages and up ladders to the very top of the ship, to the hatch where the astrogators took their star sights. The protective shield of nuclite had been rolled back and they could see into space through the clear vision port.

Rip and MacFife hurried to the side where they were connected to the Connie. Rip looked down along the length of the ship. The valve connection was in the middle of each ship, at the point of greatest diameter. From that point each ship grew more slender.

MacFife pointed to the Connie's nose. Projecting from it like great horns were the ship's steering tubes. Unlike the Federation cruiser which blasted steam through internal tubes that did not project, the Connie used chemical fuel.

"Watch," MacFife said.

There were similar tubes on the Connie's stern, Rip knew. He wondered what they had to do with the plan.

MacFife walked to a wall communicator. "Follow instructions."

He turned to Rip. "Remember, lad. The *Sagittarius* is on the other side of the Connie, about to do the same thing."

Rip waited in silence, wondering.

Then the voice horn called, "Valve closed!"

A second voice yelled, "Blast!"

A tremor jarred its way through the entire ship, making the deck throb under Rip's feet. He saw that the ship's nose had swung away from the Connie. What in space—

"Blast!"

The nose swung into the Connie again with a jar that sent Rip sliding into the clear plastic of the astrodome. His nose jammed into the plastic but he didn't even wince, because he saw the Connie's steering tubes buckle under the *Aquila's* sudden shove.

And suddenly the picture was clear. The two Federation cruisers hadn't cared about getting into the Connie ship. They had only wanted an excuse to tie up to it so they could do what had just been done.

They had sheared off the enemy's steering tubes, first at the stern, then at the bow, leaving him helpless, able to go only forward or back in the direction in which he happened to be pointing!

MacFife had a broad grin on his face. As Rip started to speak, he held up his hand and pointed at a wall speaker.

The Connie commander came on the circuit. He screamed, "You planned that! You—you—" He subsided into his own language.

Galliene's voice spoke soothingly. "But my dear commander! How can I apologize enough? Believe me, the man responsible will be reward—I mean, the man responsible will be disciplined. You may rest assured of it. How unfortunate! I am overcome with shame. A terrible accident! Terrible."

MacFife picked up a microphone. "Same here, Connie. A terrible accident. Aye, the man who did it will hear from me."

"It was no accident," the Connie screamed.

"Ah," Galliene replied, "but you cannot prove otherwise. Commander, do you realize what this means? You are helpless. Interplanetary law says that a helpless spaceship must be salvaged and taken in tow by the nearest cruiser, no matter what its nationality. We will do this jointly, the *Aquila* and the *Sagittarius*. We will take turns towing you, my friend. We will haul you to Terra like any other piece of space junk."

MacFife could remain quiet no longer. "Yes, mister. And that's no' the end o' it. We will collect the salvage fee. One half the value of the salvaged vessel. Aye! My men will like that, since we share and share alike on salvage. Now put out a cable from your nose tube. I'll take ye in tow first."

He cut the communicator off, and met Rip's grin.

The two spacemen had figured out the one way to repay the Connie for his attempts on the asteroid. They couldn't fire on him, but they could fake an "accident" that would cripple him and cost Consops millions of dollars in salvage fees.

Nor would Consops refuse to pay. Salvage law was clear. Whoever performed the salvage was not required to turn the ship back to its owners until the fee had been paid, in whatever currency he cared to specify.

And there was another angle. The cruisers would tow the Connie into the Federation spaceport in New Mexico. If past experience was any indication, the Connie would lose about half its crew—perhaps more. They would claim sanctuary in the Federation.

Rip shook hands solemnly with the grinning Scotchman. It would be a long time before Consops tried space piracy again.

"We'll be back at our family fight again tomorrow," MacFife said, "but today we celebrate together. Ah, lad, this is pure joy to me. I've had a score to settle with yon Connies for years. Now I've done it."

He put an arm around Rip's shoulders. "While I'm in a givin' mood, which is not the way of us Scots, is there anything ye'd like?"

Rip could think of only one thing. "A hot shower. For me and my men. And will you take the prisoners off our hands?"

"Yes to both. Anything else?"

"We'll need some rocket fuel. Terra says we have to correct course. Also, we'll need a nuclear charge to throw us into a braking ellipse. And we need a new landing boat. The sun baked the equipment out of ours."

MacFife nodded. "So be it. I'll send men to the asteroid to bring back the prisoners and your Planeteers." He smiled. "We'll let yon rock go by itself while hot showers and a good meal are had by all. It's the least of what ye've earned."

Rip started to thank the Scot, but his stomach suddenly turned over and black dizziness flooded in on him. He heard MacFife's sudden exclamation, felt hands on him.

White light blinded him. He shook his head and tried to keep his stomach from acting up. A voice asked, "Were you shielded from those nuclear blasts?"

"No," he said past a constricted throat. "Not from the last. We got some prompt radiation. I don't know how much."

"When was that? The exact time?"

Rip tried to remember. He felt horrible. "It was twenty-three-oh-five."

"Bad," the voice said. "He must have taken enough roentgens of gamma and neutrons to reach or exceed the median-lethal dose."

Rip found his voice again. "Santos," he said urgently. "On the asteroid. He got it, too. The rest were shielded. Get him. Quick!"

MacFife snapped orders. The ball-bat would have Santos in the ship within minutes. Being sick in a space suit was about the most unpleasant thing that could happen to anyone.

A hypospray tingled against Rip's arm. The drug penetrated, caught a quick lift to all parts of his body through his bloodstream. Consciousness slid away.

CHAPTER NINETEEN

SPACEFALL

Rip was never more eloquent. He argued, he begged, and he wheedled.

The *Aquila's* chief physician listened with polite interest, but he shook his head. "Lieutenant, you simply are not aware of the close call you've had. Another two hours without treatment and we might not have been able to save you."

"I appreciate that," Rip assured him. "But I'm fine now, sir."

"You are not fine. You are anything but fine. We've loaded you with antibiotics and blood cell regenerator, and we've given you a total transfusion. You feel fine, but you're not."

The doctor looked at Rip's red hair. "That's a fine thatch of hair you have. In a week or two it will be gone and you'll have no more hair than an egg. A well person doesn't lose hair."

The ship's radiation safety officer had put both Rip's and Santos's dosimeters into his measuring equipment. They had taken over a hundred roentgens of hard radiation above the tolerance limit. This was the result of being caught unshielded when the last nuclear charge went off.

"Sir," Rip pleaded, "you can load us with suppressives. It's only a few days more before we reach Terra. You can keep us going until then. We'll both turn in for full treatment as soon as we get to the space platform. But we have to finish the job, can't you see that, sir?"

The doctor shook his head. "You're a fool, even for a Planeteer. Before you get over this you'll be sicker than you've ever been. You have a month in bed waiting for you. If I let you go back to the asteroid, I'll only be delaying the time when you start full treatment."

"But the delay won't hurt if you inject us with suppressives, will it?" Rip asked quickly. "Don't they keep the sickness checked?"

"Yes, for a maximum of about ten days. Then they no longer have sufficient effect and you come down with it."

"But it won't take ten days," Rip pointed out. "It will only take a couple, and it won't hurt us."

MacFife had arrived to hear the last exchange. He nodded sympathetically. "Doctor, I can appreciate how the lad feels. He started something and he wants to finish it. If y'can let him, safely, I think ye should."

The doctor shrugged. "I can let him. There's a nine to one chance it will do him no harm. But the one chance is what I don't like."

"I'll know it if the suppressives start to wear off, won't I?" Rip asked.

"You certainly will. You'll get weaker rapidly."

"How rapidly?"

"Perhaps six hours. Perhaps more."

Rip nodded. "That's what I thought. Doctor, we're less than six hours from Terra by ship. If the stuff wears off, we can be in the hospital within a couple of hours. Once we go into a braking ellipse, we can reach a hospital in less than an hour by snapper-boat."

"Let him go," MacFife said.

The doctor wasn't happy about it, but he had run out of arguments. "All right, Commander. If you'll assume responsibility for getting him off the asteroid and into a Terra or space platform hospital in time."

"I'll do that," MacFife assured him. "Now get your hyposprays and fill him full of that stuff you use. The corporal, too."

"Sergeant," Rip corrected. His first action on getting back to the asteroid would be to recommend Santos's promotion to Terra base. He intended to recommend Kemp for corporal, too. He was sure the Planeteers at Terra would make the promotions.

The two Federation cruisers were still holding course along with the asteroid, the Connie cruiser between them.

Within an hour, Rip and Santos, both in false good health thanks to medical magic, were on their way back to the asteroid in a ball-bat boat.

The remaining time passed quickly. The sun re-

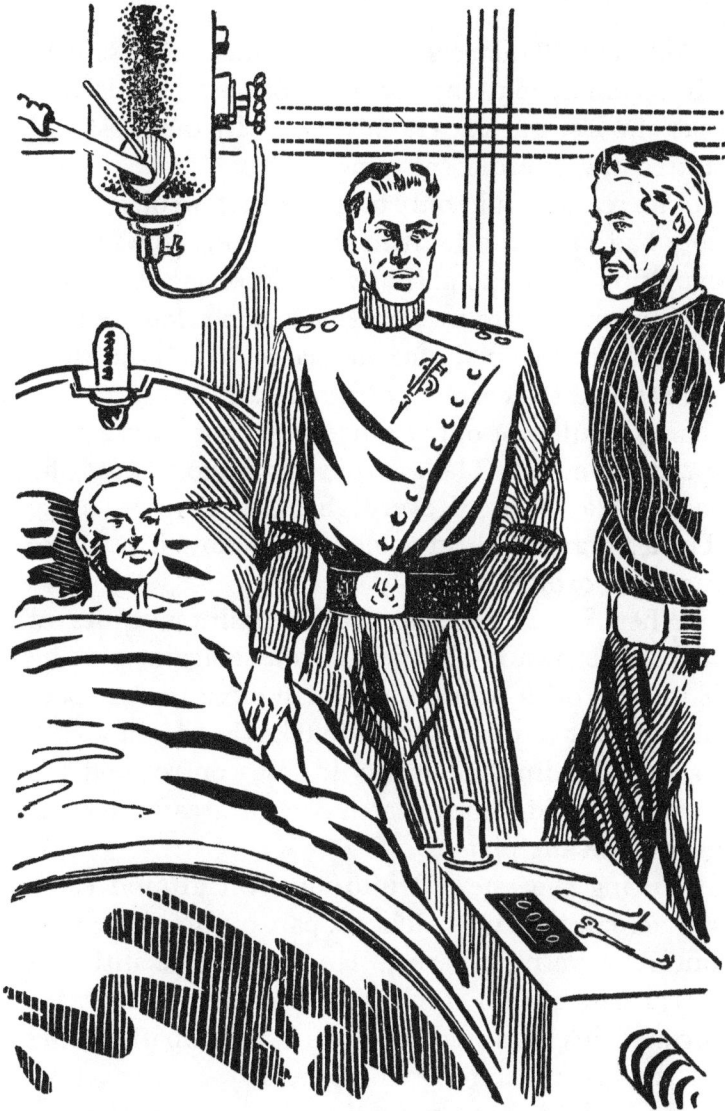

"Let Him Go Back to the Asteroid, Doctor."

ceded. The Planeteers corrected course. Rip sent in his recommendations for promotions, and looked over the last nuclear crater to see why the blast had started the asteroid spinning.

The reason could only be guessed. The blast probably had opened a fault in the crystal, allowing the explosion to escape partially in the wrong direction.

Once the course was corrected, Rip calculated the position for the final nuclear charge. When the asteroid reached the correct position relative to earth, the charge would not only change its course but slow its speed somewhat. The asteroid would go around the earth in a series of ever-tightening ellipses, using Terra's gravity, plus rocket fuel, to slow it down to the right orbital speed.

When it reached the proper position, tubes of rocket fuel would change the course again, putting it into an orbit around the earth close to the space platform. It wasn't practical to take the thorium rock in for a landing. They would lose control and the asteroid would flame to earth like the greatest meteor ever to hit the planet.

Putting the asteroid into an orbit around earth was actually the most delicate part of the whole trip, but Rip wasn't worried. He had the facilities of Terra base within easy reach by communicator. He dictated his data and let them do the mathematics on the giant electronic computers.

He and his men rode the grav planet past the

moon, so close they could almost see the Planeteer Lunar base, circled Terra in a series of ellipses, and finally blasted the asteroid into its final orbit within sight of the space platform.

Landing craft and snapper-boats swarmed to meet them and within an hour after their arrival the Planeteers were surrounded by spacemen, cadets from the platform, and officers and men wearing Planeteer black.

A cadet approached Rip and looked at him with awe. "Sir, I don't know how you ever did it!"

And Rip, his eyes on the great curve of earth, answered casually, "There's one thing every space-chick has to learn if he's going to be a Planeteer. There's always a way to do anything. To be a Planeteer you have to be able to figure out the way."

A new voice said, "Now that's real wisdom!"

Rip turned quickly and looked through a helmet at the grinning face of Major Joe Barris.

Barris spoke as though to himself, but Rip turned red as his hair. "Funny how fast a man ages in space," the Planeteer major remarked. "Take Foster. A few weeks ago he was just a cadet, a raw recruit who had never met high vack. Now he's talking like the grandfather of all space. I don't know how the Special Order Squadrons ever got along before he became an officer."

Rip had been feeling a little too proud of himself.

"It's good to get back," Rip said.

CHAPTER TWENTY

ON THE PLATFORM

There were two things Rip could see from his hospital bed on the space platform. One was the great curve of earth. He was anxious to get out of the hospital and back to Terra.

The second thing was the asteroid. Spacemen were at work on it, slowly cutting it to pieces. The pieces were small enough to be carried back to earth in supply rockets. It would be a long time before the asteroid was completely cut up and transported to Terra base.

Sergeant-major Koa came into the hospital ward and sat on Rip's bed. The plastifoam mattress compressed under his weight. "How are you feeling, sir?"

"Pretty good," Rip replied. The worst of the radiation sickness was over and he was mending fast. Here and there were little blood stains just below the surface of his skin, and he had no more hair than a plastic ball. Otherwise he looked normal. The stains would go away and his hair would grow back within a matter of weeks.

Santos, now officially a sergeant, was in the same condition. The rest of Rip's Planeteers had resumed duties on the space platform. He saw them frequently because they made a point of dropping in whenever they were near the hospital area.

Koa looked out at the asteroid. "I sort of hate to see that rock cut up. There isn't much about a chunk of thorium to get sentimental over, but after fighting for it the way we did, it doesn't seem right to cut it into blocks."

"I know how you feel," Rip admitted, "but after all, that's what we brought it back for."

He studied Koa's brown face. The big Hawaiian had something on his mind. "Got vack worms chewing at you?" he asked. Vack worms were a spaceman's equivalent of "the blues."

"Not exactly, sir. I happened to overhear the doctor talking today. You're due for a leave in a week."

"That's good news!" Rip exclaimed. "You're not unhappy about it, are you?"

Koa shrugged. "We were all hoping we'd be together on our next assignment. The gang liked serving under you. But we're overdue for shipment to somewhere, and if you take eight weeks' leave, we'll be gone by the time you come back to the platform."

"I liked serving with all of you, too." Rip replied. "I watched the way you all behaved when the spaceflap was getting tough and it made me proud to be a Planeteer."

Major Joe Barris came in. He was carrying an envelope in his hand.

"Hello, Rip. How are you, Koa? Am I interrupting a private talk?"

"No, Major," Koa replied. "We're just passing the time. Want me to leave?"

"Stay here," Barris said. "This concerns you, too. I've been reassigned. My eight years on the platform are up, and that's all an instructor gets. Now I'm off for space on another job."

Rip knew that instructors were assigned for eight-year periods. And he knew that the major's specialty was the Planeteer science of exploration. Barris's specialty required him to be an expert in biology, zoology, anthropology, navigation and astrogation, and in land fighting. Not to mention a half dozen other lesser things. Only ten Planeteers rated expert in exploration and all were captains or majors.

"Where are you going?" Rip asked. "Off to explore something?"

"That's it." Major Barris smiled. "Remember once I said that when they gave me the job of cleaning up the goopies on Ganymede I'd ask for you as a platoon leader?"

Rip stared. "Don't tell me that's your assignment!"

"Almost. Tell me, would you recommend any more of your men for promotion? I'll need a new sergeant and two more corporals."

Rip thought it over. "Koa can check me on this. I'd suggest making Pederson a sergeant and Dowst and Dominico corporals. Kemp and Santos already have promotions."

"That would be my choice, too," Koa agreed.

"Fine." Barris tapped the envelope. "I'll correct the orders in here and recommend the promotions. We'll get sixteen new recruits from the graduating class at Luna and that will complete the platoon I'm supposed to organize. Two full platoons are waiting, and the new platoon will give me a full-strength squadron. Except for new officers. How about Flip Villa for a platoon commander, Rip?"

Rip knew the Mexican officer was among the best of his own graduating class. "I have to admit prejudice,"[1] he warned. "Flip is a pal of mine. But I don't think you could do better." His curiosity got the best of him and he asked, "Can you tell me what this is all about?"

Joe Barris reached over and rubbed Rip's bald head. "By the time fur grows back on that irradiated dome of yours, I'll be on my way with Koa, Pederson, and the new recruits. Santos and the rest of your crew will report to Terra base. Flip Villa will join them there. You'll be on earth-leave for eight weeks, but it will take about that much time for Flip and the men to assemble the supplies and equipment we'll need."

He pulled a sheaf of papers out of the envelope. "Koa, here are orders for you and your men. They say you're to report to Special Order Squadron Seven, on Ganymede. SOS Seven is a new squadron, the first one organized exclusively for exploration duties, and I'm its commanding officer. Koa, you'll be my senior noncommissioned officer. I want you and Pederson with me because you can organize the new recruits enroute. They have a lot more to learn from you than they got in their two years of training. You'll make real Planeteers out of 'em."

He picked a paper from the sheaf and waved it at Rip. "This is for you, Lieutenant Foster." He read, "Foster, R.I.P., Lieutenant, SOS. Serial seven-nine-four-three. Authorized eight weeks' earth-leave upon discharge from hospital. Upon completion of leave subject officer will report to Terra base for transportation to SOS Seven on Ganymede."

Joe Barris handed Rip his new orders. "You'll be on the same ship with Flip Villa and your men. Flip will be another of my platoon leaders. I'll be waiting for you on Ganymede. The moons of Jupiter will be our home for quite a while, Rip. Our first assignment is to explore Callisto from pole to pole."

Rip didn't know what to say. To serve under Barris, to have his own men in a regular squadron platoon, to have Flip Villa in the same outfit, and to be assigned to exploration duty—dirtiest but most exciting of all Planeteer jobs—it was just too much. He couldn't say anything. He could only grin.

Major Joe Barris looked at Rip's shiny head and chuckled. "From what I hear of Callisto, we're in for a rough time. Your hair will probably grow back just in time to turn gray!"

WHITMAN BOOKS
FOR BOYS AND GIRLS

NEW STORIES
OF ADVENTURE AND MYSTERY

Up-to-the-minute novels for boys and girls about favorite characters, all popular and well known——

ROY ROGERS and the Rimrod Renegades
ROY ROGERS and the Gopher Creek Gunman
ROY ROGERS and the Raiders of Sawtooth Ridge
ROY ROGERS and the Outlaws of Sundown Valley
ROY ROGERS and the Ghost of Mystery Rancho

GENE AUTRY and the Big Valley Grab
GENE AUTRY and the Bad Men of Broken Bow
GENE AUTRY and the Thief River Outlaws
GENE AUTRY and the Redwood Pirates
GENE AUTRY and the Golden Ladder Gang

TARZAN and the City of Gold
TARZAN and the Forbidden City

THE BOBBSEY TWINS: Merry Days Indoors and Out
THE BOBBSEY TWINS in the Country
THE BOBBSEY TWINS at the Seashore

WHITMAN BOOKS
FOR BOYS AND GIRLS

NEW STORIES
OF ADVENTURE AND MYSTERY

THE WALTON BOYS in High Country
THE WALTON BOYS in Rapids Ahead
THE WALTON BOYS and Gold in the Snow

SAND DUNE PONY

RIP FOSTER Rides the Gray Planet

TOM STETSON and the Blue Devil
TOM STETSON and the Giant Jungle Ants
TOM STETSON on the Trail of the Lost Tribe

GINNY GORDON and the Mystery at the Old Barn
GINNY GORDON and the Mystery of the Missing Heirloom
GINNY GORDON and the Disappearing Candlesticks

TRIXIE BELDEN and the Gatehouse Mystery
TRIXIE BELDEN and the Red Trailer Mystery
TRIXIE BELDEN and the Secret of the Mansion

ZANE GREY'S The Spirit of the Border
ZANE GREY'S The Last Trail

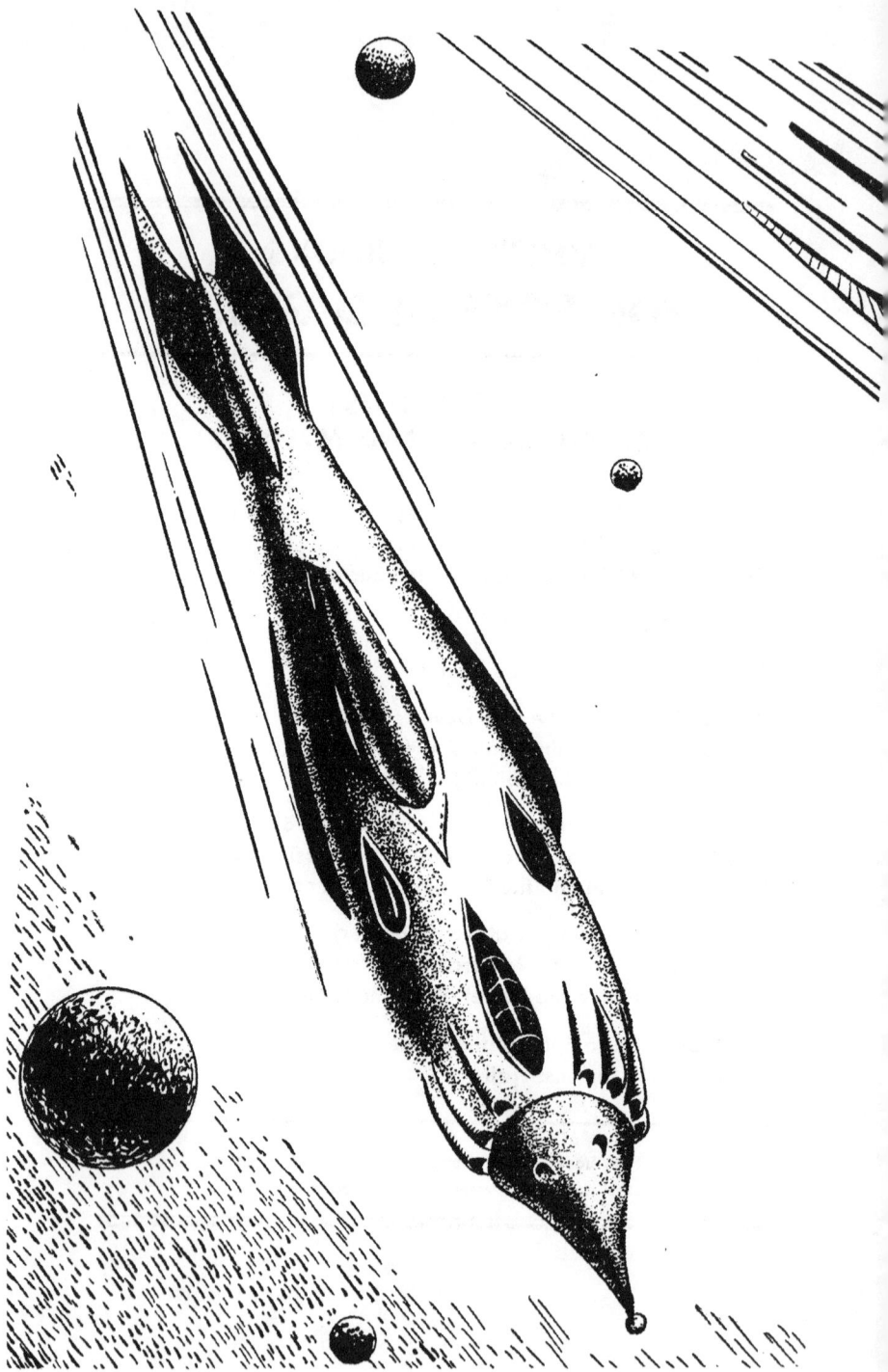

www.ingramcontent.com/pod-product-compliance
Lightning Source LLC
Chambersburg PA
CBHW031152270326
41931CB00006B/237